THE 3 Rs

Copyright 2011 of the individual pieces with the individual authors

Blackberry Writers:

Pat Doona

Mary Finnegan

Ann Martyn

Marie Meagher

Bernadette McQuaid Murphy

Guest Writers: Brendan Finnegan

Donal Finnegan

Maura Burke

Published by: The Blackberry Writers

Email: blackberrywriters@gmail.com

ISBN: 978-0-9569242-0-9

Printed and bound by: Standard Printers, Galway

GW00418411

Acknowledgements:

Blackberry Writers would like to thank the following:

Glenamaddy Credit Union.

Mai Murray, Active Retired Association, Glenamaddy for planting the idea of a writers' group in Glenamaddy.

Mary Donnellan, Glenamaddy Library for hosting our launch.

Mary Petit, Glenamaddy Community Centre for providing our first "home".

Photograph Acknowledgements

Ann Martyn

Padraic Finnegan

Claire Cunniffe, secretarial support

Standard Printers, Galway

A special word of thanks to all those whose sponsorship was received subsequent to the book going to press.

Contents

INTRODUCTION

History happens in the way ordinary people act and react to events in their lives.

The three Rs, Rhyme, Rhythm and Reminiscence is recalling a way of life lived by the writers; their experiences and observations.

Social history is still in its infancy. Writing from the heart and the head, the Blackberry writers' speak quietly, using simple language, in narrative and poetic form, using rhyme, rhythm and humour in their reminiscence. Their voice is fresh, vibrant and personal with no rehashing of old stories.

The 3 Rs gives insight into a period of history from 1944 to 2011. It gives interesting and significant details which will bring the past alive for readers.

As readers there is nothing better than when you connect with moments in a book. When reading the 3 Rs I hope that something strikes a chord, with you, the reader.

When growing up the 3 Rs reading, (w)riting and (a)rithemetic were considered and still are the fundamentals of a basic education. The 3 Rs for the Blackberry writer's rhyme, rhythm and reminiscence are the fundamentals for the stories and poems in this anthology.

The Blackberry Writers' is a fledgling group of (for now) female writers who came together early this year. They meet in Glenamaddy once a week facilitated by Bernadette McQuaid Murphy. As a facilitator from the very beginning it was obvious that these ladies had something special. They had lots to say which is great when facilitating a new group.

This is their first book but I have no doubt we will hear from them again.

Thank you for purchasing a copy and "doing your bit" to keep the creative flair alive in rural areas. Enjoy!

Bernadette McQuaid Murphy

THE 3 Rs

MEMORY LANE

I'm going down memory lane

I'll only stop to pull a tráneen

I'll leave the door open for a "whileen"

I won't be long – You come too.

I'm going down familiar fields and roads

Where slow munching cows circle around

And birds converse with the sweetest sound

I won't be that long – You come too.

BLACKBERRIES

Blackberries are very juicy
Blackberries are very sweet
The fruit of the bramble
Such a tasty treat to eat

Blackberry pie is divine
Blackberry wine is wicked
The brier extracts a heavy fee
Blood and torn flesh its penalty

Blackberry ink so artistic
Blackberry maggots so atrocious
Lithe arching barbed stems
Graceful curve with jagged rim

Blackberry converted from fruit to phone
Blackberry links up the worldwide web
Quill and ink transformed to twitter
Links from Iron Age Woman to Obama

The Blackberry is an edible fruit but it is not a true berry, botanically it is termed an aggregate fruit, composed of small droplet. That's the science bit over. The blackberry conjures up all sorts of conflicting images, lovely yummy blackberry jam on crusty bread, hot blackberry and apple pie smothered in cream, torn flesh and blood from briers, wriggly white maggots hiding in dark fruit, blackberry smart phone keeping you in touch with your friends.

When we were trying to come up with a name for our writing group, all sorts of suggestions were coming up, images connected with writing, quills and pens and all kinds of everything. We wanted something to connect back to the past as all of the group had stories of their childhood. We also wanted something connected with our modern everyday life, so what is the modern version of the quill... the blackberry, that's our version and we are sticking to it. During our national school days there was always a story in our Irish books where the family went out picking the sméara dubha.

When the bog body of Iron age Haraldskaer Woman was discovered in Denmark in 1977 traces of blackberries and millet were found in her stomach. So we know that people have been eating blackberries for at least 2,500 years. Down through the ages blackberries have been cooked in dishes from jam to pies to pickles to blackberry wine. They are now found in the freezer sections of supermarkets on their own, or as part of mixed berry selections that are buzzed into smoothies.

It can be dangerous work picking blackberries because the lovely juicy ones always seemed to involve having to manoeuvre your way into the thicket of brambles, usually ending up with bloody blackberries. I remember one time when our cousins were home from Nottingham and we all went down the fields to pick blackberries. Our cousin Josephine was in charge of the blackberry gathering operation, my brothers Michael and Thomas, my cousin Bernadette, my sister Mary and I were the blackberry picking operatives. When Jo called a halt to picking and we all brought back our berries to be put through quality control under her inspection she declared that we had collected more maggots than blackberries. She is still involved in the food industry today. I wonder does she ever make blackberry (and maggot) pie.

Blackberries grow both wild and cultivated worldwide. They tolerate poor soil and colonise wastelands. The State of Oregon in the USA is one of the biggest producers of blackberries but Mexico and Serbia are not far behind. Blackberries grow throughout the world, they grow in both the Northern and Southern hemispheres and are so invasive that they are considered a serious weed in many places. It is both a vicious and beautiful plant, it will cut your flesh with its prickles and here is another science bit, the blackberry bramble doesn't have thorns… it has prickles. Same difference to anyone who has been cut to bits by it.

It is also a beautiful plant from the time its five white or pale pink petals turn first into green fruit then red and the saying goes "when the blackberry is red it's still green" and finally to its ripe sage of black fruit. The blackberry leaves turn the most beautiful shades of yellow, russet and red in Autumn.

We have all heard the African American folktales of Brer Rabbit who lived by his wits and cunning in the Brier Patch. These tales were compiled by Joel Chandler Harris and published in book form in 1881. Uncle Remus is the fictional negro character telling the tales which were collected from negro slaves in the Southern States of America. The same tales had been part of the Cherokee culture, long before Joel Harris started collecting the tales in the 1870's, so the prickly briers have featured in folk tales for ages.

Barack Obama made world news shortly after he was sworn in as the President of the United States when he refused to surrender his Blackberry to the secret service, now the humble old blackberry was making world news but as a communication tool not an ingredient for jam.

Of course all blackberry loving people especially if you live in England know you are not supposed to pick blackberries after Old Michaelmas Day, October 11th because after that date the devil goes out and urinates on the leaves. However, in Ireland we could pick blackberries for a little longer if the weather was dry but never after Halloween, because on that night the fairies travelled around the highways and byways and the wee folk did a little wee wee on the blackberry fruit so it was no longer safe to eat after that. There is indeed truth behind those legends because after the middle of October when the weather is cooler and wetter the fruit becomes infected by moulds and could prove to be toxic

Níl aon tinteán mar do thinteán fein. There is no fireplace like your own fireplace. This is an old Irish saying and one that I tend to agree with.

Sitting by the fireside in my big comfortable armchair I look into dancing multicoloured flames, one white, one yellow and a multicoloured sequence of red to yellow to orange, radiating warmth and comfort as I sip my cup of green tea.

Perfection!

After a while the heat recedes and it's feeding time for the fire again. I arise from my chair, go to the wicker basket, piled high with long peaty sods of turf. This turf – stuff of the earth – feels crackling dry and surprisingly light for its size. I take two sods at a time and feed the hungry hearth until the fire is replete. The heat fades until the new material sparks to life and soon become multicoloured flames again. I gather the residue of turf mole, tiny particles of turf that have fallen on the hearth in front of the fire, with my well worn shovel and brush, deposit this into the fire where it disappears into the hungry flames.

I return to my comfortable haven and soon become flushed by the warmth of the open fire. I doze off and my dream takes me to the early 1970's when I was in Worthington's bog with my father and brother. In order to obtain fuel for heat and cooking it was necessary to cut turf. Turf and timber were the stable diet of our fireplaces. We had four fireplaces. One was in the kitchen, one in each bedroom and one in the parlour. The kitchen held a yellow Stanley range with four iron feet to support it (our cat took up residence under the range and had to be forcibly removed from his hot house every now and again to see the outside world). It seemed that the fire in the box of the range never went out. It was steadily fed by day and raked at night (damp sods of turf were deposited to slow the fire down). The first job every morning was to put dry sticks and little bits of turf on the fire and rekindle it until it burst into flame again and provided enough warmth to boil the kettle and boil an egg for my father who had to leave the house at 7am to cycle to work. The fires in the bedrooms were only lit if the temperature was below zero. The parlour fire was lit only for visitors and at Christmas.

Sometimes during the month of May, depending on weather conditions, my parents decided it was time to start cutting the turf crop that would be used the following winter. The first job was to clean the bank. This involved cutting away the top layer of heather and moss – it could be three to four feet deep – to get to where the turf started. My father used a slane – a spade like instrument with a wing – to cut sods of turf. As he lifted the slane he threw the sod of turf to my brother, who expertly caught it and placed it neatly on a wheelbarrow, placing one sod beside the other until the base of the barrow was full and then stacked upward until the barrow could hold no more. Then he had to wheel the barrow about fifty yards away and slide the full load off in a little pile where it was left to dry in the wind and sunshine. While my brother was gone with one load I was on hand to repeat the same process, catching the wet yet surprisingly solid sod of turf that my father throws to me and placing it on my barrow until it is full. I wheel it away to tip its contents beside the last load. This relay continues between my brother and me keeping my father in a steady rhythm of work until tiredness sends us home. We continue this daily ritual until the task is complete.

After some time and many wistful looks towards home, not to mention many tummy rumbles, our mother arrives with the "tea". This tea consisted of a bottle of tea with milk and sugar, some homemade soda bread, buttered with homemade butter, some cheese or tomato and hard boiled eggs. This feast was devoured with much appreciation and we dined in the bog The taste and texture seemed to be intensified by the clear bog air and sheer hunger after our exertions. I had time to wander about and explore the area. There was one spot in that bog with a water spring. The water was always ice cold and drinking it was very refreshing. My Dad told me that this water could not be boiled. Further on there was an area of greenery on a raised bank. Underneath this green foliage I found, to my delight, a myriad of berries. These berries were called moonogues. They were very dark coloured with a tinge of blue. I had forgotten all about them, until a few years ago I saw blue berries in the supermarket, I could not believe my eyes, as they looked the same as the wild berries I collected and enjoyed, mashed with sugar, as a child.

When the turf had time to dry a little the next step in the process of turf rearing was tossing (scattering out) the piles of turf earlier deposited from wheelbarrows. This enabled each sod to dry independently and completely. Then the turf had to be footed (put into little piles). Then it was left to season (get very hard and dry) until it was time to take it home, back then it was a donkey and cart.

I have to tell you about our donkey called Ned. Ned was a work shy donkey. Each morning when he was required to pay for his keep he would see my brother coming into the field, bridle in hand, and our Ned would turn tail and run to the far end of the field to avoid capture. A merry dance would ensue and through tender and not so tender words Ned was cornered and bridled against his wishes. If my brother decided to ride on Ned's back on the journey back to the house Ned would make every effort to dislodge his unwelcome passenger. He would run near the hedge and under low hanging branches hoping my brother would be toppled. When none of his antics worked he resigned himself to a day of cart pulling. He enjoyed being pampered by ourselves with various titbits of food from the kitchen table. We would always make sure he got oats and apples and the carrot tops and sometimes we would smuggle the full carrot into his mouth. For dessert he would have bread and butter. He just loved bread and butter!

When Ned was tackled and the cart put on his back my brother and I would jump into the empty cart for the one mile journey to the bog. Pat had the enviable task of being able to remain standing in the cart, reins in hand, as he expertly held his balance as it bounced and jolted about the road. I on the other hand had to sit on the floor and hold onto the side for dear life. Oh how I envied him his sea legs.

When we arrived in the bog the cart was parked beside the footings of turf and we fitted it into the cart where it arrived with a great thud. We worked steadily until we could not get any more turf on the load. Then we walked home, Pat at Ned's head guiding him with the bridle and I usually behind the cart scuffing the ground as I went. When the journey to and from the bog was travelled a few times Ned knew the drill, I might add he always seemed more anxious to get home than to set off for another load. I often thought you could let him off on his own and he would take all the right turns to get there and back unaided, if only we could train him to fill the turf into the cart!

Harvesting the turf was a very long and labour intensive operation. It started in May and usually ended in September when it was transported home via donkey and cart and stacked in a shed close to the house, ready for use.

To augment the turf and make it easier to light the fire it was necessary to collect sticks. This was one of the jobs laid out for me when I came home from school. I would walk around the ditches where the trees grew and salvage wind blown light branches. We called these light sticks kippens and they provided excellent kindling for the fires.

There are two types of bog. One is a Blanket bog (see note*)
The other is a raised bog (see note**).

The method of cutting and harvesting has been improved and a lot of the work is now mechanised.

Our bog is a Raised bog and is home to a rich variety of flora and fauna. Every Spring the turf cutting machine arrives in the area and cuts predetermined amounts of turf for each bank owner. We order 11 hoppers – that's a lot of turf when you're saving it - but in a harsh winter it disappears very swiftly. A hopper is about 90 metres long and 8 sods wide. When the turf is newly cut its consistency is about the same as dough, and like dough bakes into a cake, turf bakes in the sunshine and becomes hard and firm as it dries. When the top of the turf is dry it is time to turn it over in order to dry its underbelly. When it is dried it is put into footings by hand (usually my husband's) as this kind of work is not at all popular with this generation of youth. When it is fully dry it is taken home with a tractor and trailer and stored in a shed near the house, where it is readily available when required.

I reflect on the process that has taken place to ensure this luxurious winter warmth and marvel at how much things have changed and how little they have changed. Turf is still cut in this area and I now use it as the main source of heating in my own household. I love the earthy spicy smell it exudes as it generates warmth and welcome to one and all.

In recent times there has been great controversy regarding the EU banning of turf cutting in certain bogs in Ireland. Many people who have harvested turf for generations were rightly upset. As a result of this a campaign was launched to save our turf cutting rights. We now have TDs in Dail Eireann who have been elected on the stance they have taken to back the cutting of turf in this area and we secured a Government promise that turf cutting can continue for domestic purposes.

I awake from my slumber and contemplate the flames, and I think that the back breaking work of last Summer has been very rewarding.

*Blanket Bogs

These can be defined as bogs which form in areas where relatively high levels of rainfall occur annually. They are found mainly on the lowlands in the western counties and also on mountain areas throughout the country. They are shallow bogs which form a blanket-like layer over the underlying soil. Their average depth is 2.6 metres.

**Raised bogs

These can be defined as bogs which form from vegetation that grows due to the nutrients present in rain water.

In Ireland Raised Bogs occur mainly in the central areas where moderate amounts of rainfall occur annually. They develop and form on top of fens. They have a dome-shaped surface and are very deep in some areas where depths of over 13 metres have been recorded. (This includes the depth of the underlying fen).

- And ** downloaded form Bord na Mona website.

SAVED BY THE BELL

It was stifling hot. Over thirty young girls were squashed into the senior classroom of the convent school, where fifth and sixth class pupils were taught by the school principal, Sister Agatha. She turned her back to the pupils and started writing furiously on the blackboard.

"Ciúnas (Quiet), she said.

The whispering stopped immediately. Silence filled the room, except for the yellow faced clock on the back wall that drummed out a quiet defiant rhythm, tick....tock....tick....tock. The only other sound to be heard was the occasional screech of chalk as it careered across the black writing board.

Dry white dust filled the air. Sunshine through the west windows caught dust particles and created bands of dancing light that settled on the wooden floor. Around the side walls, yellowing pages of old maps were suspended on metal hooks, faded and worn almost beyond recognition. Two pupils shared each desk and the attached bench. These were made from solid oak, built to withstand the ravages of time. The upper surface of the desk contained small indentations for pencils or nib pens and two ink wells, which were protected by sliding brass covers.

The well scrubbed school girls sweated in their navy serge pinafores, white blouses and knee length woollen socks. Some shifted uneasily on the old wooden benches. But the heat scarcely registered with one child in particular. She had a lot more to struggle with that Summer afternoon. The Irish language class had commenced and eleven year old Josephine Conroy, sitting in the back row, knew from past experience the terror which was about to be unleashed.

Sister Agatha loved the Irish language with a passion. It was our heritage and our responsibility to hand it on to future generations. She was fond of repeating to anyone who would listen. She believed that every child, without exception should be able to speak the native language fluently. This was her individual crusade for Ireland and she used whatever means she could to ensure success. Her missionary zeal was never doubted by her past and present pupils.

With the blackboard covered with writing, the nun finally turned towards the class. She wore a black habit – the religious robes of the community to which she belonged. It was a uniform reminiscent of female clothing from the middle ages and consisted of a long pleated black ankle length dress, with wide full sleeves and a black underskirt. Large wooden rosary beads were attached to a black leather belt worn around her waist; they clattered as she moved. Her forehead, neck and the upper bodice of her dress were concealed by a stiff white wimple. A black veil covered her head and extended beyond her shoulders.

It was Sister Agatha's practice to get each pupil to read from their textbook. Josephine trembled as she was picked from the group. Her fear of reading aloud, words which held no meaning, led her to inevitably stumble over the pronunciation. Repeated efforts seldom improved so that she was always punished. This day would be no exception.

With quiet deliberation the nun removed her wooded stick from its hiding place behind the blackboard and placed it on her desk. It was a long, flat piece of wood, smooth on both sides. In the past, it was used to add strength and stability to a window blind. Now, it was a grim warning of the consequence of failure.

"Seas suas (Stand up)."

This instruction, given by Sister Agatha, was understood and obeyed. Josephine stood in the narrow space between the bench and the desk and opened her school book at the correct page. The large black letters filled the page.

"Léigh o liné a dó (Read from line two)."

"Ghlaoch sé amach go hard (He called out loudly). Ni raibh sé in am an doras a oscailt ar aon chor (He could not open the door at all)."

She read the first sentence without error, but the words blurred together and she stumbled painfully over the pronunciation. In the next sentence "Ar aon" became "Aaron" (A name from the bible).

"Léigh é arís (Read it again)." It was the same result.

"Arís (Again)."

This time the instruction became a roar. Josephine tried once more. She knew it was coming.

Now.

Three quick strides and Sister Agatha reached the back of the classroom. She raised the wooden cane and cracked it loudly upon the small desk. The force caused Josephine's pencil to hop off the desk onto the floor. Maura Murphy, in the desk beside her, cowered in her seat.

"Hold out your hand Josephine".

The nun caught her trembling hand and raised the cane once more. Just then the school bell sounded, indicating the end of classes for the day. Distracted, the teacher lowered her stick and moved to the top of the class. She hid the cane out of sight behind the blackboard.

Sister Agatha stood and faced the class once more. With her head bowed she blessed herself and joined her hands piously, as she led her pupils in evening prayers.

"Class dismissed girls," she said.

In the last row at the back of the classroom, Josephine Conroy sat abruptly. She bent to retrieve her pencil, then noticed the wet puddle around her feet.

Acknowledgements

With sincere thanks to Bernadette and Páid for the Irish translations.

WAR TIME MEMORIES

I was four when World War II started in 1939. I remember the Anderson shelters the Council gave each house to put up in the back garden. We had one. The family dug a large hole eight feet wide by eight feet long and eight feet deep. The Council put concrete around the sides and at the bottom, then fixed a heavy duty galvanised top made of iron or steel, I cannot remember which now. We hardly ever used ours because when there was heavy rain it would fill up with water, and we had to wait for a man with a stirrup pump to come and empty it out.

People called World War II "the Phoney War" at first as it seemed to take a long time to start.

We would go to the public shelters on the corners of main roads at night before each raid started. We would go early to get a good place to sit or lie down on the concrete floor. Some people brought blankets and pillows and a few lucky ones brought mattresses. The children went first, and the Mams and Dads if they weren't in the forces, would come after the pubs closed. There would always be someone with an instrument and we would have a sing song. The women and older girls would bring knitting. They knitted socks, gloves and scarves for the forces.

I remember one night when we were at home in bed and the sirens went off at two in the morning. There hadn't been a raid for some time before so we stayed at home. The sirens were situated on each factory roof and air raid wardens (R.A.P.W.) would operate them when they saw a plane. We got up and ran down to the shelter in our back garden even though it had water in it. We became aware that our step-father was missing. My sister went back into the house and found him trying to get out of the wardrobe. He was shouting that he couldn't open the door to the bedroom. Needless to say he had been to the pub.

Each evening as it got dark we would close the black-out curtain so no light would penetrate outside. Woe betide any house with a light shining. The warden would bang on the door and shout, "Don't You Know There's a Bloody War On?"

Westminster (the Parliament) decided instead of one hour Summer time we would have two hours, and us children would not go to bed because it was still light at eleven o'clock.

We would hear the planes coming over but could not tell the difference in the sounds. We did not know whether they were friend or foe. You could hear the whistle as a bomb fell. Our house was in a road that had railway lines either side. The enemy would make for the lines and more often than not hit the house.

The big shops in town set up emergency hospitals in their basement, as the hospitals could not cope with all the wounded as well as carrying out their usual work.

Towards the end of the war the Germans made a bomb with its' own engine. You could hear it coming, throb, throb, throb. Then the engine would stop, and whistle as it dropped and blew up. That was the most terrifying sound. We called the bomb a Doodlebug.

When the food rationing started we would join a forming queue, even if we didn't know what the queue was forming for. It could be for an orange per ration book or a half pound of sausages. Mom would hide fruit so we would all get our share, but more often than not they would not be found until they were rotten.

We were allowed a quarter of sweets a month. If you had hens you got corn instead of eggs. The Council put bins in the streets so anyone with food to throw away could put it in the bin for the pigs. They would be collected once or twice a week.

Even clothes and shoes were on coupons. It was good if you worked on the trams or buses or the railway as you were given a uniform every year and boots.

People who worked nights never knew if the house would be there next morning. The gas, electric and water would be off half the time with a standpipe for water.

I'm not absolutely sure but I think rationing went like this: 2oz of tea, 2 oz of margarine, 8 oz of sugar, one rasher of bacon, one egg and half pound of meat. Bread and milk had to last you a week per person.

Vegetables weren't rationed if you could get them. Most families dug up the garden or had an allotment that they would work on Sundays. Bread and milk floats were pulled by horses. There would be hell to pay if the horse went to the toilet in the road at one house and someone else had to shovel it up. Coal was rationed. The older boys would walk the railway lines picking up lumps of coal that had dropped from tram engines while the firemen were shovelling it into the fire box.

I was nine years old when the war ended but we still had to fetch coke from the gas works six miles away. We used an old pram to transport it, one load in the pram and another load in a sack on top of the pram. At first Mom and I would go for it but as I got older I had to go alone before school. Often a wheel would come off the pram and I had to rely on the goodwill of a passer by to help and put it back on.

When the war ended the whole street got together and had a street party. The children played games like the sack race and egg and spoon (using a stone) race. We sat at long tables and had a tea party. Someone wheeled out a piano and other instruments. There were barrels of beer.

In London, the King, Queen and Churchill stood on the balcony waving to the crowds. The two princesses put on headscarves and joined in with the dancing in Trafalgar Square. The Royal Family never left London during the war even though Buckingham palace got bombed.

JANEY MACK

Musha Katie how are ya?

Janie Mack Bridie, is it yourself? Ara shure I'm only middlin Bridie. I'm comin from the hospital after spending half the night up there with "Thomasheen Kelly" I have a reel in my head with tiredness.

Go way.

Shure as I'm standin here Bridie. Poor old devil, our Larry found him down at the cross last night and he ravin. He was drownded to the skin and he blatherin all sorts. He was only wearin his long johns and Wellingtons. He didn't say "yes", "aye", or "no". I don't think he knew who he was.

What time was that Katie?

Latish Bridie, gone eleven anyway.

Go way Katie, your Larry must have got an awful fright.

He did Bridie, faith he did, but fair play to him he rang the Doctor and the Priest from his mobile and then ourselves. They got him back to the house and got him warm, then we had to wait on the ambulance. It took two hours to get there, the lads were thinking of drivin in themselves we were that long waitin.

Ah now Katie.

Then in hospital there were no beds so they left him on an oul trolley and the poor cratur trying to get off it, looking for his mother he was and no staff to stay with him but what could I do Bridie but stay.

Still twas good of ya Katie. Ah God help him. His poor mother would turn in her grave if she seen him, so she would. What age would Thomaseen be?

He wouldn't be seventy yet Bridie. He started getting the pension a few years ago alright. I used to see him in the butchers every Friday and he buying the best of mate for himself. They asked me that up in the hospital too, his date of birth, shure I hadn't a clue. Talk about forms.

What'll happen to him now Katie do ya think?

Well between you me and the wall, if he pulls through I'd say he'll go into a nursing home. Shure what else, he couldn't go back up to that house and no one to mind him or anything.

And he used to keep that place spotless. Do you remember the day of the station.

I do indeed. A grand place he had, but it's gone to rack n'ruin.

Go way. He mustn't have been feeling himself for a whileen, otherwise he's have been tidying and painting and cutting the grass like he used to. I knew I hadn't seen him at mass for a good while but I didn't want to be nosy and go askin, you know.

Aye, everythin thrown about inside and things growin wild outside. The two poor ould dogs were sleeping below in one of the bedrooms. Mind you they weren't starving or anything. My lad brought them up to our place. Two lovely dogeens they are.

Father Carty was saying last night that he was up to see him on the first Friday and that he seemed to be his usual self.

God help him and he with no one belonging to him here and his only sister in England. She'll have to come home now anyway.

They're trying to get howld of her now.

Things must be serious so Katie.

I suppose.

I haven't seen that wan in years.

Whist will ya. She was always a right oul Biddy. Bad cess to her.

You can say that again.

One never knows Bridie, do they?

Faith we don't, and you know aren't we as well off not to.

The priest might want a hand cleanin the place up a bit later on Bridie, would ya be able?

Shure, no bother. Just give me a ring.

Thanks and if ya see any of the others ya might ask them for me. I'm going to go now, me head is pounding and I'm dying for a drop of tae.

TRIGGER

Soulful eyes
Face so grave
Understanding each move I make
Tail wagging
Ears upright
Knowing when to sit and stay
Always happy
Never snappy
Every time I glance your way
Yet when the Postman comes to call
To deliver bills into the hall
You howl, bark, show your teeth
But I tell him you're gentle underneath
But he – he darts away in fright
Escapes to his van with delight
And I – I look into those eyes
Gentle, loving and wise
And wonder why
My faithful friend, my buddy, my pal
Could be feared by any man.

THE RISING OF THE BREAD

The advantages of home baked bread are widely known. The baking of good brown bread involves skill and experience. Baking bread was very much part of the daily routine in Irish kitchens, and still is in many. Mostly it was the women of the house who did the baking but men who lived alone were very good at it too. I remember one elderly man that baked his bread on a griddle. This was an iron type of hot plate with a handle either side that produced a flat circular type bread. He had a shop in the room just off his kitchen and you could get the beautiful smell of the bread baking while in the shop.

In secondary schools in Ireland in the seventies girls took a subject called Domestic Science, more aptly named today as Home Economics. It entailed cookery, needlework and theory. It was during one of my first classes of Domestic Science that I tried my hand at baking bread.

Each week we prepared a different dish, sometimes on our own and sometimes with another student. We brought the ingredients from home and if you forgot any or all of the ingredients you got a right ear bashing. Some girls' eggs got broken in transit on the school bus. If they were lucky enough to have pocket money and had Domestic science in the afternoon they'd buy an egg down town at lunch time to avoid the fuss.

As a first year the first dish I prepared was soup, pretty straightforward, nothing much could go wrong with that I hear you telling yourself, and nothing did go wrong. The second dish was brown soda bread. I was a little worried about this, shop bought bread was used mainly at home and I had little experience baking bread. I duly brought in the ingredients and set to work putting my self-doubts on the "back burner".

I spent the first fifteen minutes weighing the ingredients meticulously, sieving them into the heavy, yellow mixing bowl, rubbing the margarine in, mixing and kneading and cleaning up as I went along. When all this was done and a circular shape of dough had formed I finished by cutting a sign of the cross into the top of the dough. It was believed that no bread would bake well unless it was cut with the sign of the cross.

The next step was to transfer the dough onto the already warmed baking tray without dropping it! and then with a massive sigh of relief "popping" it into the pre-heated oven for a specific length of time. If you're still with me you'll have guessed by now baking wasn't really "my thing".

The routine in the school was that we left our dish in the kitchen and collected it on the way home when it had cooked. Often they wouldn't be ready by the time class was over so the teacher would take them out and leave them at our pre-determined work stations.

The domestic science kitchens were in "the tech" (Vocational School) on the Marian road, Boyle near St. Mary's college. The Mercy convent school was on the Carrick road about a ten minute walk away. After collecting our dish we caught the bus home from the college.

We were happy about this because we were guaranteed a seat. Other days being a first year you were one of the last to get on the bus, and had to either stand until some people got off or squeeze into a seat with two others.

The smell of the fresh bread in the kitchen that Autumn afternoon when I rushed in out of breath, both from the exertion of hurrying and the excitement of another day over was delightful. I pulled off the tea towel in anticipation and looked down. I automatically paused and stared. My bread was brown, it was round with a perfect sign of the cross but it was as flat as a pancake. Red faced with disappointment and embarrassment I stuffed it in my bag and ran for the bus.

My first priority was to get a window seat so I could stare out and not have to make eye contact with anyone, as by this time the hot tears were threatening. I was twelve years old, a few weeks off my thirteenth birthday. What went wrong? I asked myself. I went back over in my head every step I had taken, and then I went over it again.

"How would I show it to my sister and mother?" I wondered as the bus meandered down the Sligo road, around by the picturesque Rock of Doon before turning right for Corrigeenroe. At that time although I lived only five miles from the school, the bus took the "scenic route". By the time we came into Knockvicar I had sort of worked out what had gone wrong. I must have forgotten to add the baking powder, the raising agent.

The raising agent produces a gas within the mixture and when it is heated in the oven, the gas expands and rises, pushing up the mixture and giving the bread a nice texture. Air is another raising agent used in baking. Either I had not introduced enough air when sieving the flour or when rubbing in the margarine or I had forgotten to add the baking powder.

My bus stop was Rockingham gates. I used to leave my bicycle there. From the bus stop I cycled along the main Boyle Carrick-on-Shannon road, turning right at Ardcarne up the Croghan road that leads to Easternsnow. As I took the corner that blustery bad tempered Autumn evening (which matched my own temper perfectly) the herd of cattle were lowing loudly in the field on my left, they probably thought I was coming to feed them. It suddenly dawned on me what to do with the "bread".

I dismounted, grabbed the still warm offending object and gave way to my frustrations by tearing it into little pieces. Then I slung them bit by bit and with force over the barbed wire fence to the cattle. The cattle stood staring but stopped lowing. Without a backward glance I pedalled at speed home.

On reaching home everything was as normal. Heat radiating from the range with a plethora of cats, at different stages of the sleep cycle under and around it, dinner on the table and a general enquiry as to how my day went. Call it mothers intuition if you want but my mother never enquired about the bread and in true pre teenage fashion I didn't reveal any of the details.

It was many years later before I plucked up the courage to bake another one, this time though with a little more success. Over the years I have baked plenty of different breads and cakes disaster free with the help of the "just add water" mixes from the supermarkets (Thank you whoever had the foresight to invent same) I can see you all shaking your heads but as I told you earlier baking was never "my thing".

The memory of that Autumn evening remains fresh and powerful in my mind and whenever I drive along that road now on my way to Ardcarne graveyard, to the church in Cootehall or to visit my sister in Carrick-on-Shannon I think of my "bread" and have a good laugh.

MONDAY WASHDAY

A working mother,
Up to her elbows in suds,
pummels dirty clothes,
One more Monday chore complete.

A flying line of clothes,
billow in the wind,
Children run between white sheets –
Rickety line falls –
sheets no longer white.
Children flee from reprimand.

Weary woman sighs,
remembering times long past.
Girl with golden curls,
dancing through white sheets.

GOD, HENS AND TD'S ACCORDING TO DAD

What is God? God is a Mighty Man.
I think the first question in the little pink catechism we used at national school was Who is God?
God is the Father, the Son and the holy Spirit or words to that effect; my brother Michael had no problem remembering that answer.
The second question was, What is God? God is Almighty. Alas, Michael couldn't remember the word almighty, no matter how many times my mother tried to teach him his catechism, the almighty word wouldn't' enter his brain. My father would immediately pipe in with, "Just remember God is a Mighty Man" probably thinking this word association would help Michael remember the word almighty. Did it help Michael remember? Well, sort of... from that evening onwards, whenever Michael was asked What is God? The answer came back instantly; God is a Mighty Man and that is the answer he always gave when asked in school, much to his teacher's dismay. To this day "God is a Mighty Man" is still a catchphrase in our family.

My Dad, Tom Hannon was a great source of information to us children, however his tendency never to let the truth ruin a good story meant we often acquired misinformation rather than information. My younger brother Tomas, aged about four, attempted to grow hens. Dad had told him that if he planted feathers he could grow hens. Thomas collected some good strong feathers and he carefully planted them in the back garden. He sat watching them for a while and throughout the evening he went out to check on the feathers every few minutes. Then he came excitedly racing into the house to tell us that his hens were starting to grow and come outside quickly so we could see them growing. The evening breeze was stirring the feathers; Thomas was waiting for them to pop up out of the ground at any moment. Dad not wanting to disappoint Thomas told him "sure enough, that's a sign that the hens are growing underground but it will take them a few months before they are strong enough to come out of the ground". The village well was located at the end of our garden and Thomas had planted the feathers alongside the path to the well and within a day or two some of our neighbours while drawing water managed to step on the feathers and crush them. Thomas was very annoyed that we didn't get to see his hens grow. However, we were able to watch chickens grow into hens during our childhood years. If you wanted chickens in those days they would arrive by bus. Women including our Mum could be seen collecting boxes of fluffy yellow chickens from the bus at the Square in Dunmore.

Dad was responsible for a number of other morsels of misinformation in our childhood. We spent many long Summer days trekking down our fields, wading across the river, walking through more farmland to get to Barrett's Wood to search for Robin Hood. It would have been much more straightforward to travel to the wood by road but it was much more of an adventure to trek cross-country. Dad having spent time working in Nottingham loved telling us the story of how he met Robin Hood in Sherwood Forest outside Nottingham, and he had told him that sometimes during the Summer he came over to Dunmore and hid out with his merry men in Barrett's Wood. The reason we never found them we were told was because they were dressed in Lincoln green and blended in with the woodland, so it would be impossible for us to see them.

Politics is always a topic that fascinates Irish people and as children we were fascinated by politics thanks to Dad. We thought it would be great to go to Dublin and get into the Dail to see the TD's working. Not that we had any great interest in the structure of the government but when we had asked Dad what kind of work TD's did , he told us that "they sat in the Dail talking all day but saying nothing" we really wanted to go and see this awesome sight.

Dad loved nature; he shared and imparted his knowledge and love of the natural world to us. We spent happy days hiding in the fields waiting for rabbits or foxes to appear, and my younger sisters Mary and Breda, spent many hours running after rabbits trying to shake a grain of salt on their tails, so they would be able to catch that exact rabbit again. Of course Dad had given them this information. I don't think they ever managed to catch a rabbit for the first time so their chances of catching it the second time were non-existent, but the effort they put into chasing them kept them fit. In later years his grandchildren walked those fields with him listening to his "rabbit tales". Dad loved talking, it was his main pastime, and he loved talking so much that it scared people from walking past our house (which was located on a crossroad) if they happened to be in a hurry to get back home. Going "round Killooney" is a popular walk with many people and as soon as evening drew in Tom Hannon was always outside sweeping leaves, weeding or clipping the hedge so he could pounce on anyone passing by his house for a chat.

I recall one trip my brother Michael and I made with Dad to Corcoran's Mill in Adrigoole; our flighty pony Charlie was drawing the cart with the grain in it. A long laneway led down to the mill, Mick Corcoran ground the corn for the local farmers and then it was loaded back onto the cart. Mick Corcoran having the gift of the gab himself, was quite content to stand at the large opening upstairs in the mill, and shoot the breeze with Dad. Michael who spoke in a very quiet tone of voice kept tugging at Dad saying, "Daddy, Daddy I think we should go" "We'll go in a minute Michael said Dad and continued to talk to Mick. "Daddy, I think Charlie wants to go". "Sure we'll go in a minute Michael, the grass near a river is very sweet, Charlie is in no hurry to leave he's enjoying eating it" and back to his conversation. Then Mick Corcoran points out into the twilight and says, "What in the name of God is that speeding down the road". Dad straining to see across the fields said "It's a pony and cart heading towards the bridge, Jaysus, tis speeding alright, I can't see anyone with it", Michael raised his voice at this point and shouted "It's Charlie, I was trying to tell you he wanted to go and you wouldn't listen so he just went himself". Time, tide and Charlie waited for no man. Dad dashed down the steps, no time to go back up the lane, just a mad dash across the fields with us following. Luckily there was a long steep hill before we reached home, this slowed Charlie down and Dad caught him.

He took us out on Winter nights telling us about the stars and once we were lucky enough to see the magical spectacle of the Aurora Borealis, clouds of light rolling around the sky also known as the Northern Lights. Dad's explanation; it was caused by the angels in heaven having a wrestling match. Walks at night in the bog or near damp ground he had us watching out for Will-o'-the-Wisp, the little magical elf who was always out with his lantern searching for something. That was a much more wonderful explanation for this phenomenon than the oxidation of phosphine or methane. One night as Dad and my sister Breda turned down into the Killooney road in the car, standing before them in the centre of the road was an owl. Breda still remembers the feeling of awe as they both got slowly out of the car and stood observing the owl from within a few feet. Dad conveyed facts about owls, while the owl stood unperturbed observing them for a number of minutes, before taking off into the silent night sky.

Our Dad always seemed to have a great love of animals including the cattle on the farm and he would compose poems about the cows that we loved to hear. His own Dad died when he was twelve and it wasn't easy for his mother to bring up three children on a small farm in the 1930's. His younger brother Michael and Hugh went on to higher education, but although Dad had to leave school to take over the running of the farm he read voraciously and expanded his knowledge on many subjects. He absolutely enjoyed a course on trees and woodland he attended in NUIG along with my sister Breda, telling everyone he was now going to University. He would add on a magnitude of extra information on trees each night before the class concluded; luckily the lecturer and class appreciated this addendum. My Dad's Uncle, John Donelon, from Lerhin also had a great love and communication with nature and this knowledge must have come down through the generations. Once walking through the fields in Lerhin with John my Dad told us how they encountered a fox, John put his hand on my Dad's shoulder to make him stand still. The fox and John seemed to instinctively communicate with each other, standing still for a few moments before each moved off in opposite directions. "That fox is not from around here, he has a bit to travel yet before he gets to where he is going" said John as if this encounter was the most natural thing in the world and the fox had just whispered that information to him and they just continued with their walk.

After my Dad died in 2002 a blackbird appeared in our home place, he used to peck at the window and generally hang around outside, he was around the place from first light to night. When our mother moved a short distance down the road to my brother Thomas' house the blackbird moved there also. We all decided this was a sign sent by our Dad that he was now contentedly connected with nature and wanted us to know that. Mum decided to name the blackbird Tom and everyday when she went outside and called Tom, the blackbird immediately flew down and stood at her feet. One day Mum was showing her grandchildren how the blackbird Tom would come and land at her feet when she called his name. Michael and I were watching this spectacle from the kitchen door, Michael decided to shatter our illusion that it was my Dad, "Well that's an amazing sight he said but whoever that blackbird is it's not Dad, he always disappeared down the fields whenever she went out and called him".

"Today is a gift", that is the phrase I most associate with my father. Whether the sun was splitting the stones, or the landscape was covered in snow, whether the wind was whipping through the trees or fog softly obscuring the view, Daddy would say, "Today is a Gift".

Yesterday is History
Tomorrow is a Mystery
Today is a Gift
So embrace the present

We engraved the above quotation on his headstone after his death; we thought our version of this well known verse was very appropriate for him, recognizing his love of nature and poetry.

MODES OF TRANSPORT

Sitting thinking the other day, it occurred to me that I have been the recipient of many varied modes of transport in my life, so far.

My first mode of transport was a pram. While I don't remember being transported in it, I do remember the pram. It was in my house for many years, unused, until I grew old enough to use it to transport my baby (doll) around and play at being a "Mammy". I was the youngest of the family so there was no other sibling vying for its accommodation. This pram had four big spoked wheels, a handle that rose gracefully out of the main body which was made of a sturdy material and a hood that could be raised and lowered, depending on sunshine or lack of it. Inside there was a very thin mattress of spongy material. The mattress was covered with a pillow case which nearly fit. One day I came home from school and found my pram had been converted into a trolley for milk cans. It had been re-engineered to the extent that all I could identity was the wheels and handle. For many years it was used to convey milk cans to the pick up point, about a half mile from the house, where it was transported by tractor and trailer to the local creamery.

When I was about five years old my parents decided it was time that I started to attend mass on a regular basis. The town and church was about one mile away. My mother always attended 8.30am mass on a Sunday morning. She attended this mass because back then if you wanted to receive communion you had to fast from the night before. She would cycle there and back. By the time she got home my father would have the breakfast ready. I am sure she needed it by the time she got home, around 10.00am. The Sunday breakfast was indeed a very pleasant experience. I would awake to the smell of rashers, freshly cut off the side of bacon. This aroma would always entice me out of my warm bed. I would get dressed as quickly as I could and arrive in the kitchen to see my father adding tea to the pan where onions sizzled and bubbled in the tasty gravy he had created. There would also be a fried egg if required, and during the Summer he had a great knack of finding mushrooms on his early morning stroll through the fields. All this would be added to the fry and we ended up with a luscious plate of food.

After breakfast he and I would get ready for mass. We donned our best clothes, freshly polished shoes from the night before. On Sundays he wore his hat. The method of transport used was his bicycle. This bike was no ordinary bike. Most children were conveyed on the carrier of their parents bike. It was not like that for me. No, my dad had a bike with a carrier on the back and a big square parcel carrier attached to the front. He hoisted me onto the front carrier and away we went. His chin was just above my head as he peddled up and down hill and flat to get us there on time. It was a wonderful seat to have. My view of the world took on a whole new prospective as I glided by and the countryside became a blur. I was flying through the air with my feet dangling one each side of the front wheel. On and on we went until we arrived outside the church and parked the bike beside a myriad of other bikes, of all shapes and sizes. Then my Dad would greet various neighbours and friends as they converged on the church.

When I was about ten years old, my parents bought our first car. It was a black Ford Anglia. This car was used only for my father's work. We still walked or cycled to mass or the shop. I remember we talked my mother into trying her hand at driving the car. She was a somewhat nervous passenger which did not augur well for her driving prowess. However we persisted until she said she would give it a go. There was one proviso – the only way she would sit behind the wheel was if we pushed the car so that she could get the feel of driving and gain confidence. We pushed the big monstrosity getting up a head of steam comparable to a very slow stroll. My mother let out a loud yell to slow down as she could not stop the car. I remember laughter sapped our strength and the car ground to an abrupt halt. My mother's driving career ground to an equally abrupt halt.

The next family car was purchased some years later. It was a red Mini. Don't get me wrong a mini is a lovely car but I am yet trying to discover the reason why a man of 6ft 1" and broad with it would buy a mini. It is one of the smallest cars available. I have seen him performing acrobatic acts when trying to get out of it. The seats were very low to the ground, my father was not getting any younger, and the head room was non existent. He had to put his hand on the roof for leverage as he put one leg out on the ground then his behind followed and finally his left leg. He then stood beside the car and straightened his contorted body into its natural form again.

I learned to drive in that car. I remember the first lesson I had. It was on the way to the bog on a very quiet road. My Dad told me what to do and when to do it. I still remember the thrill of it as I actually succeeded in getting the car to go forward without conking out. After the first few lessons I used to drive the car out our little side road and reverse back over and over again until I was as good at reversing as going forward. By the time I was seventeen I had grown competent and was able to apply for my driving licence and get insured on the mini. I was then able to take my mother shopping or do odd journeys as required.

When I was eighteen, the mini was sold and replaced by a Ford Escort. The Escort was a very fine car with lots of power (compared to the mini). I remember bringing it for a spin on the main road and putting my foot down. Boy did it respond, it leaped to life and surged forward giving me the feeling of unlimited power.

I met my husband when I was nineteen. Back then he was driving a Honda 50. I became a pillion passenger complete with my own helmet – supplied by him. He upgraded to a Honda 175. This bike was much more powerful and we were able to travel to further places. The first trip on the Honda 175 was to Galway, a mere forty miles away. We mounted up and arrived in Salthill about one and a half hours later. When I dismounted I will never forget how my legs felt like they had a life of their own as my knees had turned to jelly and I had to walk like John Wayne. I thought I would never recover and dreaded the thought of the return journey.

When we parked the bike we had the problem of what to do with the helmets to keep them safe. We soon came up with a solution. We went to the local church, helmets in hand, and deposited them in the safety of the confessional box. The problem arose when we returned to retrieve them, mass was on, the church was packed. We had to sit on the steps outside until it ended and everyone departed, we were hoping that the priest had not heard confessions that particular morning.

The day we got married we owned an Opel Kadette. I say We as on that day everything he had became mine and visa versa of course. For our departure from the reception the car was decorated with shaving foam and confetti with hearts and slogans and there were a few tin cans and a chamber pot tied onto the back.

For our honeymoon we had booked a holiday in Italy. This necessitated air travel, something new to both of us. We boarded the plane and took our seats. We blessed ourselves as we sped down the runway and prayed as we climbed vertically into the sky. By the time the plane levelled off and our ears stopped popping, we relaxed and enjoyed the rest of the journey until it was time for touch down. We landed at the airport and skipped along the runway until the roar of the engines seemed to slow the plane and finally come to a stop. When I alighted on to firm ground again I almost kissed the earth Pope John Paul style.

GENTLEMEN OF THE ROAD

Tramps, vagrants, journeymen with a trade, wandering bards, all known as gentlemen of the roads were a regular feature of life in the forties, fifties and sixties.

It was a tough way of life but a chosen way of life for them. Apart from their name and habits, little was known about them, and their life before they "took to the roads" and their reasons for doing so remained a mystery.

They usually travelled alone and had a preferred route. They had a way of sharing information with each other as to whether a house was friendly or not. Again this was a mystery. They slept in barns and were fed by households. They were on the whole an intelligent bunch, some of whom enjoyed a wide ranging conversation while others were reserved. They were always polite and thankful.

One man I remember used to come up our road about once every six months. He used to look in the "pig bin" for food. This was during the second world war when people were asked to put their unwanted food and leftovers out for the farmers once or twice a week so that they could give it to their pigs.

This particular man never asked or begged for food. He would chop wood, cut grass, fetch water from the well. Depending on the season he would pick fruit or potatoes and do other jobs for farmers to earn money.

He had long grey hair that he would tie back with a bit of string and a beard. He was always clean in appearance. People gave him clothes and boots and sometimes he would wash his clothes in a stream.

He like all "gentlemen of the road" never stopped anywhere long and never gave any notice of his planned departure. One morning on wakening you would discover he had gone and that would be it until he appeared again "out of the blue".

EASTER BLESSING

"Did you see my gloves anywhere Catherine?" Aunt Margaret asked her niece, as she quickly attached her hat to her wispy grey hair with a large hat pin. She looked critically at her reflection in the hall mirror. Her small navy hat with its neat veil was her latest purchase from Arnotts millinery department late last year. It was a suitable hat, she decided to wear today to Easter Sunday Mass.

"Don't forget the bottle to collect Easter Water," Catherine reminded her aunt, as she found her gloves beneath the scarves on the hall table. Margaret thanked her as she picked up her prayer book and the bottle, placing them both in her handbag. She blessed herself with holy water from the small font behind the front door and quickly left the house. The parish church was already crowded even though she had arrived early for the eight o'clock mass.

Last Sunday was Palm Sunday, when the branches of the palm tree were blessed. Afterwards, as was the custom, she had collected a small branch from the basket at the entrance to the church. This would be used later with holy water to bless their home. The branch was placed above the Sacred Heart picture in the kitchen for the coming year. The presence of the blessed branch was believed to prevent calamities upon the household.

Margaret squeezed into a pew near the side alter and knelt to say her novena prayers before the parish priest appeared from the sacristy. Finally, the long homily was ended, the holy water was blessed and mass finished with the prayer to St Michael the Archangel.

Margaret waited until the church was almost empty before collecting the holy water, then quickly made her way home for breakfast. It was a long overnight fast for an old person, if they wished to receive communion the following morning at Mass.

"Any new style in the church for Easter?" Catherine asked. It was a common joke between them that Margaret paid more attention to the parishioners than the priest. They chatted about the new clothes that their neighbour Maura and her daughter were wearing. Her sister Biddy was in America and she often sent home large clothing parcels for the family. "You should have seen what your wan was wearing. She was as big as the back of a bus in the yellow costume.

Catherine was clattering pans on the Stanley range as Margaret entered the kitchen. Soon the smell of cooking rashers and sausages permeated the house. Margaret was a poor cook, but her self appointed job was boiling the kettle and making tea at mealtimes. With her task completed she covered the teapot with the old knitted tea cosy, before she sat down to breakfast with Catherine.

Afterwards, as Catherine continued her tasks about the house she placed the holy water bottle in the press in the upstairs parlour. She knew that later on Aunt Margaret would sprinkle holy water to bless the house for the coming year.

It was late afternoon Easter Sunday when Catherine returned from a walk with her friends. As she opened the front door she was assaulted by the smell of poítin. Aunt Margaret answered her call from somewhere upstairs. She appeared, standing at the top of the stairs with a large bottle in her hand. Oh Lord, Catherine thought, dismayed. Had her aunt finally succumbed to the family failing for alcohol? She had been abstinent all her life.

"Aunt Margaret, what on earth are you doing?" Margaret looked at her niece puzzled.

"I'm blessing the house with holy water dear" she replied, mildly. "It's Easter Sunday, you know."

Catherine looked at her aunt and grinned widely. Margaret had no sense of smell. The poítin and holy water had been in similar bottles in the press. Margaret has blessed the room with alcohol.

CHILDHOOD SOUNDS

When I was a little one
The pips for the news at eight
Signalled a new day had begun
My warm bed I had to vacate.

Midday the Angelus bell that
Tolled eighteen times in all
With its, 3,3,3,9 format
Pause for prayer-the call.

In the afternoons Dear Frankie
Radio's agony aunt – her woman's page
Solved romantic matters sincerely
For listeners everywhere regardless of age.

"If you feel like singing
Do sing an Irish song"
Waltons were encouraging
On their programme of renown

Dear Sir or Madam on Saturday at seven
With John O Donoghue
Then Ceili house would end the day at eleven
Hosted by Sean O Murchu

The two Micheals on Sundays after mass
Giving us a running commentary
With passion, on every kick, puck and pass,
All for the love of the game and county.

This and more from the big box with wood surround-
Commonly known as the wireless,
No better cultural resource to be found
Instilling that sense of Irishness.

PENNY SWEETS

Moira Cooney hopped impatiently from one foot to another as she waited for a reply. Absently, Nora noticed her daughter and finally said "Yes, get tuppence from the press." Moira said a hurried thank you and turned to the old mahogany sideboard behind her. It was part of the odd mix of furniture in the living room. The surface shone with a mixture of beeswax and loving care applied each morning by her mother. Moira pulled out the old wad of newspaper that jammed the press door in position and rummaged for pennies in the shabby red purse. She quickly skipped out the back door holding the money firmly in her pocket. Nora called warningly after her retreating back, "Don't cross the road".

The main street in the village had many small shops on either side, with an equal amount of public houses. Today, there was little activity on the street, in contrast to yesterday, which was Fair Day, but the pong of cow dung still clung to the road and pavement since the fair, and Moira wrinkled her nose in disgust. On the first Tuesday of each month farmers came to the village to sell cattle. If they were successful, they would settle their accounts with the shopkeepers. Farmers paid with cash or would sometimes barter goods, such as ducks or geese, if a shopkeeper was agreeable. Their family drapery shop was busy yesterday with customers, so Moira knew it was a good time to ask for money. She was forbidden to take change from the till in the shop without permission, a good habit that was instilled in her from an early age.

She skipped towards the shop, thinking about the sweets she could buy with her money. Moira loved Lemon Drops. They were hard sweets which tingled with flavour and almost made her mouth dry if she was lucky enough to eat a few sweets together. The two pennies jingled in her pocket. She sighed happily and thought that she would have plenty to share with her friends. Clare lived in the house next to the sweetshop and Moira called for her before going into the shop.

Maddens was a small sweet and gift shop, half way up the main street. The shop window held a wonderful mixture of small figurines, matchbox toys and china dolls, placed in rows towards the front. Behind these, cardboard and tin chocolate boxes were displayed, showing pastoral scenes or cottage gardens. A large advertisement sign for Players Wills was perched precariously at the back. It served a dual purpose, providing privacy for the person behind the counter and advertising the nation's favourite cigarettes. Above the door a hand painted sign in black ornate writing proclaimed the owner's name. When Moira and Clare entered, a bell tinkled somewhere in the room beyond the shop. On her left side, behind the gift counter, a large ice cream machine hummed and shuddered before falling silent. To the right, the sweet counter was a cabinet which extended almost the length of the shop. It was taller than most of the children, but it had a glass front and the jars placed along the shelf were clearly visible. Moira pressed her face against the glass. Each jar held sweets or lollipops. Perhaps she would buy Bulls Eyes, or Peggy Legs, Sherbets or Lemon Drops.

Gabriel Madden appeared in the doorway. He was a portly man, with much evidence around his middle that he too loved the sweets which he sold. He waited patiently for Moira to choose from the large glass jars displayed inside the counter. Finally, she made her choice. Today she would have six lemon drops! Clare and Moira watched Gabriel. Slowly and carefully he selected a small brown paper bag from the pile on the shelf behind the counter. The bag was proving difficult to open; Gabriel licked his thumb, fumbled with the edges of the bag and finally succeeded. Next, he unscrewed the cover from the jar and dipped a white flabby hand into the lemon drops. Gabriel's fat fingers grasped a handful of sweets, he separated those stuck together and carefully counted them, before placing them in the bag. Moira thanked the shopkeeper politely and paid for the sweets. Gabriel dropped the money into a tin can behind the counter. They left and the bell tinkled once more.

Outside more children had gathered, waiting patiently. They were playing hopscotch further up the street and had seen the girls entering the shop. She offered the bag politely to Clare, Mags, Michael, Ann and Teresa. But as she raised the last sweet to her mouth, little Jimmy Clarke appeared from behind the rest of the children. "Moira, can I have a sweet too? he asked. Moira paused and looked uncomfortably at the small child. Her mother always referred to him as a bit delicate. Her last sweet, how could she part with it? Jimmy pleaded with his eyes.

"Oh" she said, reluctantly, You take it." Jimmy snatched the sweet quickly from her outstretched hand and ran behind the older children. She crumpled the small sticky paper bag in her hand. Clare, her best friend noticed. "Here" she said, "have some of mine," and taking the sweet from her mouth, she handed it back to her best friend.

WALKING AROUND DUNMORE

Caught in a dew drop
Hanging on a hawthorn branch
I see the sun rise

From Cloonkeen hilltop
Nestled in the vale below
I see Dunmore town

With proud sturdy stance
Heads held high and sombre gaze
I see dappled horses

Peake and Chequer Hills
Lead to the hamlet below
I see the Kuku

Chattering swift sprites
Under skies of sapphire blue
I see swallows swoop

Vista of the past
Wandering round Killooney
I see Corcoran's Mill

Dropping from the sky
Burning the orb of winter fire
I see the sun set

In the Sinking River
Waltzing shimmering vivid sparks
I see the stars dance

YELLOW PEAR DROPS

Yellow pear drop sweets remind me of when I was a little girl at the start of the war, when sweets were rationed. I was evacuated to Clifton, near Nottingham with the Vicar and his wife.

The travelling shop would come round once a week and stand on the Village green. A lady used to drive it and the back would open up. She would serve you from a counter. She seemed an old lady to me, but she couldn't' have been that old as she drove the van.

I went to Clifton when I was four. My sister Edna enrolled me into school in Birmingham, so I could be evacuated with my brother George. He was seven years older than me. We were sent to live in this big house. George lived in a flat above the stables with the chauffeur and his wife; I slept in one of the maid's rooms in a cot. She looked after me and of a night she got me ready for bed, she would take me along to the nursery to say good night to the children. I wasn't allowed to play with them.

I spent most of my short stay sitting in a high chair while the servants were busy. I remember I had a blue furry dog and while sitting in the high chair I decided he could do with a haircut. I don't know how I got the scissors, but I was quite happy trimming his fur, but the maid came in to check up on me and stopped me. She took away the scissors.

Another day George came in to play with me. He had got some plasticine, we made little pellets with it and were throwing them at each other but the maid came that time too. She sent him out and let me go with him into the garden.

George went to school in the village and after a while they sent me there also. There was a little girl in the same classroom. There were three classes in one room. This girl's mother owned the Post Office shop next door to the school. She was older than me and she knitted some clothes for a doll and the class gave it to me on the Friday.

Next day a big black car came to the house and I was asked if I would like to go for a ride and play with other children. They took me to Nottingham to a children's hostel. I wanted to go home and they said I had gone to live there. George came to visit me on a Sunday on a bike one of the maids lent him. I was there for about three months, then an old couple who lived opposite to the big house had me to live with them.

She was a fat little lady and he was a big man with a beard. I can't remember their names now, but they were very nice. She would wash me down each evening in a bowl on the table in front of the fire. It was a big range with hobs on either side. There was always a kettle boiling on the side. She would do the cooking on it too.

There was no running water in the house and the toilet was a shed up the garden, which he would empty when full. I couldn't reach the wooden seat, so I had a chamber pot at the side, on the floor.

I went to the school in the village and I played with the village children and then one day when I came home from school the old lady had all my clothes packed and said I was going to live at another house. That's when I went to live with the Vicar and his wife, Mr and Mrs Craig, or as I called them Aunty Agnes and Uncle Joe. I still went to the village school. I no longer played with the village children, but I could play with the children from the big house.

Opposite the Vicarage gate was an army camp and every Sunday the Vicar and I would walk in front of the marching men to church. He was also the army Padre.

I had my sixth birthday there. I remember we had a pink blancmange rabbit and Aunty Agnes and Uncle Joe gave me a doll with a china head and crock body. When I came back to Birmingham, I took it to the park and the elastic holding the limbs together broke and it all fell apart. I put it into my skirt and carried it home, crying all the way. Mom took me and it to the dolls hospital. It was a shop that repaired toys. Anyway, that was the last I saw of it. Mom said she couldn't afford to get it back. I often looked in the shop window and saw it on the shelf.

To get back to Nottingham, George still lived with the chauffeur and his wife, but not for long as George got upset. They had bought him his first pair of long trousers and wouldn't let him wear them to see Mom, so when Mom saw how upset he was, she took him home. There I stayed for the next six months.

One day while George was at Clifton when he was swimming with older children in the river Trent, a little girl was being swept by the water towards the Mill race. George swam to her and managed to save her. He was only eleven or twelve at the time.

The little girl was Doctor Legley's daughter from Bermingham. The Squire presented George with a hunting knife from the villagers and the Doctor gave him one hundred pounds which was a lot of money in those times.

As for George, he was quite a hero!

FIVE Oooo

I've reached that Five Oooo I've figured it out
It's easier to get your point across When you don't shout
Speak your mind Without saying a thing
Keep friends at a distance Let enemies in
Eat and drink as much as you can
To purge this sin I often ran
Go hiking too It will clear your head
And help you sleep when you go to bed

Don't tell the truth, if it hurts the hearer
Better to be a wheeler and dealer
When people ask how you're feeling today
Make sure they know that you're doing okay
C'os that question was never meant to be answered
So it's better to be stoic and say I'm pampered

The waist line expands, the brain recedes
I can't remember what it is that I need
When I left the kitchen and went down the hall
I knew where I was going but I falter and stall
Is it my lipstick or my brush that I seek
I return to the kitchen and try to recall
What it is that I wanted if anything at all
And to keep my sanity I have to pretend
All this exercise will reduce my rear end

Moments of madness I have had one or two
Like trying to fit into that dress of blue
And leaving the shop with an oath under my breath
Vowing even if it causes my death
I will find that perfect number
With the right size on the tag and making me look like a wonder
Now looking at my beautiful wedding dress
Wondering how was I ever that much less in size
Once again I vow to give up the rich pies

But yes it's good not to care too much
I do my own thing and as such
I find fulfilment in the simplest thing
And marvel at the birds who sing
And honeysuckle and blooming trees
The simple sound of bumble bees
Why should you whisper when you can shout
Living life to the full is what it's all about.

THE LIVING LINK

"Brostaigí" (hurry up) and "an bhfuil cead agam dul amach?", are two phrases "as Gaeilge" that have stuck in my mind since national school.

I remember as a child repeating the following two lines of poetry over and over and while not understanding them in their entirety, I understood enough to believe that there was something special at the back of the house.

"Tá tir na n-óg ar chúl an ti
tir álainn trína chéile

Recently there has been a lot of controversy regarding the teaching of the Irish in school. Different MBRI polls have drawn opposite conclusions regarding Irish adult opinion on Gaeilge becoming non-compulsory after Junior certificate. Some people don't like Irish as a language, many say this is because of the way they were taught it. They felt it was forced upon them. There is discussion currently that every citizen will have their competence in Irish assessed in the future, what this will involve or how it will be carried out remains unclear.

How Irish is taught in schools is now being overhauled. From next year there will be more emphasis on spoken Irish with the result that oral Irish exams will account for 40% of marks in state examinations and will increase to 50% in later years. The aim is to preserve and promote the Irish language and foster a love for it. Then it is believed people would be more likely to continue to speak it after leaving school.

One worrying statistic that appeared in The Irish Examiner of May 4th 2010 was that "no-showers" for the Gaeilge exam at Leaving certificate increased by 600 a year since 2006.

From general reading the consensus appears to be that there is no best way to learn a language as everyone learns differently. However, immersion is a popular way with the underlying belief that the learner gets to know the culture in which the language is spoken and gains a wider understanding.

Growing up in Ireland in the sixties and seventies snippets of Irish was always spoken in the house. We learned to speak Irish in our homes before going to school even though we were unable to write it. My mother would often end a conversation with the words "ní nach ionadh" (no wonder) and if we were bothered by something we would be told "ná bac leis" (don't mind it), it was pronounced "nabacleis". Older people regularly added a stór (treasure/darling) a leanabh (child) and a grá, (love) when talking with young people.

We had Irish words for everything. Words such as amadán (fool), ceolán (someone who was full of themselves I think), and seafóid (nonsense) were slipped into everybody's day to day conversation.

Everything or every person that was small had the suffix "een" added. This spilled over into conversation through English and we would refer to a young person as the young "oneeen" or as it was pronounced then "waneen".

When I worked and lived in London in the eighties I often used Irish words when talking with other Irish friends. When we didn't want people near us to hear what we were talking about and especially if our comments were derogatory we would revert to our "mother tongue". When out and about good looking young lads were described as "dathúil" (handsome) a comment that was followed by much giggling and looks of puzzlement from people "not in the know".

On moving to Tuam, three popular words again slipped into everyday conversation through English but with their roots very much in Gaeilge was maceen (son) this is used about and to males in general, girleen to all females and loveen to men and women, boys and girls.

The downside of the sixteen years I spent in London was that while I was able to speak individual words and odd phrases I forgot most of the grammar and now at best can only manage Gaeilge briste (broken). This saddens me as I always had a grá (love) for the language.

One of my earliest schoolbooks was called Peann agus Duch (pen and ink). In secondary school it was Peig. Peig Sayers could neither read or write Irish but dictated her autobiography about her life on the Blasket Islands to her son Maidhc File (Mike the poet) after he returned from America. It was published by Talbot Press, Dublin in 1936 and awarded the Douglas Hyde Prize in 1937. Soon after this it became a set school text for study in secondary schools. Yet seventeen year olds who have read extracts from it today have dismissed it as depressing.

Love it or hate it our native language is one of the living links between our past, the present and the future. A language of a country give its' people an identity, a sense of belonging and is part and parcel of the culture.

A MYSTERY

Call it an atmospheric illusion or what you will, you won't believe this but I have seen a leprechaun. In fact four of us saw him.

This is what took place. John my husband, myself, John's son and his school pal David who were both about thirteen at the time were on holiday at a caravan park in Killarney.

It was late afternoon on the last day of the holidays. The two boys were fishing in a river at the side of the caravan. John was watching and I was getting the tea ready. I stood at the door while waiting for the kettle to boil. I looked to my right and I saw a man about three feet tall standing or sitting on a root of a tree. If it was a Leprechaun he must have had a makeover!. He wasn't wearing a painted hat or long tailed green coat or black shoes. He had no silver buckle. He was wearing a flat cap, a sports jacket and brown cord trousers. I couldn't see his shoes because they were hidden by the grass.

He was sort of sitting forward with his feet crossed and his hands were crossed at the wrist and resting on his knees. He had a short beard. I could see him very clearly.

I called John over and asked him what he could see there. He was amazed and called the two boys over. We asked them the same question. The man never moved and had a smile on his face.

John was about to go over to him but changed his mind so I walked over to him. The closer I came to him he just faded into the background. I put my hand where I had seen him and felt a piece of moss. I asked them what I was touching and they said his shoulders.

Then I put my hand on the root of the tree and asked them what I was touching and they replied his knee.

As I moved back towards the caravan he appeared again to me. I stood and watched him until it got too dark to see.

That was thirty five years ago. I wish I'd had a camera at the time. Later when we returned to the caravan site on holiday, the site owners had cleared the river and put the residue on the side and altered the outline of the river bank.

We have told many people about it and most ask, were we at the poitín!. Writing this after all this time it is hard to believe John has passed away. His son is about forty eight and David moved on a long time ago. There is no one available to verify the story.

So, was it a Leprechaun or a small Irish man? I'll leave you to draw your own conclusions.

IRISH MOTHER

I think I'll wash his jeans still there –
the pair with the designer tear.
Lying like a discarded skin
With baggy knees, fit for the bin.

He said he couldn't take much more,
then went right out, slamming the door.
He'll wear those jeans again sometime,
to throw them out would be a crime.

I believe he didn't mean to say
Such hurtful words as he went away.
I hope he hasn't found Ann Other,
Because he's coming home to Mother!

SHEEOGUES

I grew up surrounded by superstitions.

To this day I will not walk under a ladder. If I spill salt I have to throw it over my right shoulder. I would be most unhappy should I break a mirror. I will not allow anyone to open an umbrella in the house and when I see one magpie I furtively look around for another one or two, if they don't materialise I quickly make the sign of the cross on my forehead. I believed as a child that the "good people" were always present among us and it didn't do to upset them. I suppose deep down some of those beliefs are still with me and might explain my superstitious behaviour.

Some people referred to them as "the little people" but legend tells us that they didn't like this title so most including myself called them the "good people". As I was always small in stature, five feet three without heels! I have always had a certain affinity with "the little people".

When I was growing up if you had a day when you weren't really focused on the task in hand people said you were "away with the fairies." This description was also used when describing an elderly person in a confused state.

A baby who cried a lot used to be addressed as "a little fairy", or called a changeling. This originated from a "belief" at the time that the fairies used to take babies and young children and leave a changeling or fairy in its' place.

The "good people" liked beautiful things or so I was told so we were happy enough and felt safer when we had the one dress and usually "a hand me down" at that for Monday to Saturday! Better and cleaner clothes were kept for Sunday and may explain how the saying "Sunday best" came about.

Some people dressed little boys in girls' clothes in an effort to deceive "the good people" as it was a belief that they were always on the lookout for young boys. People today would probably laugh at the idea but I read recently that there were high levels of infant death among boys as compared to girls during the nineteenth century.

As a younger girl I regularly went on picnics to the mound at the back of our house in Ardcarne. The picnic consisted of diluted Mi-wadi orange and a buttered currant bun. Doherty's bread van from their bakery in Boyle used to call every Wednesday and one of the "treats" bought was a ring of buns. I never went to the mound alone and I always left a "little gift" of a few currants for the fairies to keep them happy. The crows probably had a feast day when I left.

I loved going to the mound as a child and usually used the short-cut through the fields. Standing on that mound on a clear day, the views were exquisite. Straight ahead was

Woodbrook, to the left the Arigna mountains, behind me Grevisk and Lough Key and the plains of Boyle to the right. From what I can remember the "good people" did not mind humans visiting so long as they showed respect. Sometimes in true childish fashion we would "push the boundaries" and play a game called "King of the Castle" on the mound. This involved one of us pushing all the others down and shouting, "I'm the King of the castle, get down you dirty rascal".

Legend has it that when the first Gaels who were Sons of Mil arrived in Ireland they found the Tuatha De Danaan, the people of the goddess Dana in control of the land. The Tuatha were a short race of people. The Sons of Mil, fought the Tuatha, defeated them and drove them underground where they remain to this day in the sidhe mounds, hollow hills and plains. Ardcarne had a mound, a fairy fort and just a little further away the plains of Boyle.

It was believed that the Tuatha took their revenge for the defeat by destroying wheat and milk. Fairies were believed to have powers beyond that of humans and it was not a good idea to upset them. They crept out at night to steal from their conquerors. They were regarded as an intelligent bunch and although a distinct race they had a lot of contact with the human race.

A sudden gust of wind swirling up leaves and general debris signalled that a troop of fairies was passing by while they remained unseen by the human eye. When you went out early in the morning and saw the grass glistening with dew and it hanging on the bushes and furze you just knew that the fairy queen and her helpers had been out scattering their jewels during the night.

Milk, salt and fire are sacred in fairy lore.

As a child I was aware of three different types of fairies.

The leprechaun, the banshee and the pooka (puca).

The leprechaun was a cobbler and was in charge of guarding the treasures of the good people. I never met up with him and I never came across anyone who had their shoes mended by one either.

The Leprechaun had a reputation for being crafty and there were many stories of how he got the better of people who tried to extract information out of him as to the whereabouts of the treasure.

The banshee, derived from the Gaelic Bean Sidhe (Bean Si), woman of the fairy, or fair mounds. She is a female spirit who wails in the night to foretell disaster. She is not usually seen, only heard. People who have seen her describe her as having long streaming hair, red eyes from weeping and either a young woman or a wizened old lady. She dresses in white with a cloak and brushes her long pale hair with a silver comb. She is believed to be a spirit of earlier generations who have gone to their eternal reward who is given the task of warning.

The Banshee is seen as an omen of death, a messenger from the underworld. She is said to appear for particular Irish families with O or Mc, in their names. This always bothered me as my mother before she married and my father had surnames starting with Mc.

The pookey – (puca), comes out on November nights. They soil on nuts and berries which stops people from eating them. Some say the puca is a white horse who takes you away whether you want to go or not but will always bring you back to where you started from. Where they bring you remains a mystery to me at least.

There was a story I was told as a child which concerned a bachelor Mick Dan, who lived and cared for his elderly mother on a farmhouse according to the locals in "the back of beyond", it was so isolated. This man was "fond of a drop" and while most people gave up drink for the month of November, this particular man could never do the whole month without it.

One night on his way back from his local he was stopped by the Puca who addressed him by name. According to Mick Dan himself he was scooped up off the road and brought to every County in Connacht on the Puca. They travelled over hills and mountains at speed. When they reached a particular and well known mountain a door opened in front of them and they entered where he was welcomed "as Gaeilge" by a young beautiful girl. She thrust a fiddle into his hands and commanded him to play jigs and reels as fast as he could. For the next number of hours groups of little but very beautiful ladies danced and twirled energetically. There were no males present.

Then as the morning sun was rising in the east the Puca took the fiddle from Mick Dan telling him it was time for him to return home. The return journey was just as speedy as the first one. When this man woke up in his own kitchen around noon he found the pockets of his coat were overflowing with silver coins. From that day onwards he never touched a drop of alcohol.

I've learned recently that the great fairy King of County Galway is Finnbheara who lives outside of Tuam and loves horses. He can be seen riding a fine black horse with flaring red nostrils. He has a liking for earthly women.

ODE TO MY LAPTOP

I've gotten myself a laptop
My dream has finally come true
Blissful days googling non-stop
So many things I plan to do
A book to write my thoughts to jot
Researching and stories to plot
Everything stored in the one spot
Oh! The joy that you have brought

Now that I'm wired to the net
I've got instant info, and yet
The minutes and hours they fly by…
The family are forced to eat frozen pie
Pizza too as I click and surf
The house grows cold as I've forgotten the turf

On Line
I can read the paper or buy a car
Do the grocery shopping from afar
But where I live it doesn't pay
To deliver the goods all that way
Please somebody develop a system
That delivers food on line to my kitchen!

I'll write that book, that's what I'll do
My life my loves and family too
The things I did the joys I've had
Something tells me I'll be glad
To have this laptop to record
All this data in the format of WORD

PATTERN SUNDAY

The Pattern is a hallowed area usually around a holy well, where mass or a prayer service is held, but celebrations in these places go way back into history, into pagan festivities. The Dunmore Pattern is situated in the village of Cappagh, and Pattern Sunday falls on the last Sunday in July. The practice of going to The Pattern has died out in most areas but a few people still make a trip to their local Pattern during the last week of July.

During my childhood years I used to "go on holidays" to my aunt Kathleen O'Toole's house in Cappagh. My cousins were younger than me but there were two girls of about my own age, Phil Clarke (now Keville and still living in the area) and Dolores McCormack who lived with her Granddad in Cappagh at that time. Along with Phil and Dolores we used to take my cousins on walks and our favourite walk was "up The Pattern". On one memorable walk we took the baby Seamus O'Toole in his very heavy old fashioned pram up the bumpy, stony Pattern road. It took the three of us, assisted by Seamus's very young sisters Mary and Anne to push the pram up the "mountain" to the Pattern. The proverb tells us "many hands make light work" but many hands pushing in different directions make unwieldy work. As we rounded the last bend and had the holy well in sight we relaxed our grip on the pram. It tumbled sideways and landed on the only soft marshy bit of ground in the area. One member of our gang went running down the road shouting that we had drowned the baby while the rest of us rescued the blasé baby. There was a lot of watercress, rushes and moss under the pram but as it was the middle of Summer the amount of water in the vicinity wouldn't have quenched the thirst of a midge, much less drown a pretty hefty baby. Seamus was rescued and he is now a fine specimen of a man living in Cappagh with his wife Sally and his gang of teenagers and never displayed any sign of post-traumatic stress after this incidence.

The Pattern always fascinated me, and I collected information on it for an article in our local Dunmore newsletter some years ago. The last Sunday in July is held in special regard in many parts of Ireland. It is known as Garland Sunday in some places and as Pattern Sunday in other areas. It is also Reek Sunday when people from all parts of the country climb Ireland's holy mountain in Co Mayo, Croagh Patrick, better known in the West as the Reek.

The Gaelic festival of Lunasa was held at this time of year. Festivities included feasting, idolization, dancing, debauchery and fighting. With the establishment of the church, clergy made valiant efforts to discontinue these heathen rituals. But, rituals ingrained in the culture and hearts of the people were hard to eradicate. In the early 11th century the Synod of Bishops were threatening people with harsh penance for excesses. The hierarchy tried to stamp out the pagan festivals but the local clergy worked out a better compromise, they began to merge the pagan celebrations with celebrations of local holy days and local saints feast days. For the celebration of Luanasa, local clergy often independent of the organized Catholic church introduced mass or prayers on Pattern Sunday.

Pattern Sunday or Garland Sunday was celebrated in most parts of Ireland and all seemed to follow the same type of ritual. Early in the day the religious ceremony was held and "doing the rounds" was part of this ceremony.

Once the religious part of the ceremonies were over in the late afternoon or early evening, ambience began to change, things began to hark back to pagan times. Stalls were set up and my grandfather remembered that one of the items being sold on the stalls in Cappagh were gooseberries. Faction fights were a regular occurrence at this stage and he also recalled groups of men coming from somewhere in Mayo and faction fights taking place, I think these faction fights were more for entertainment than contention. Later in the evening things became more cordial between all gathered there, dancing took place well into the night. There was a triangular clearing just above the well in Cappagh known as "Cnoic an Damhsa" where dances were held. A piper is said to have played at many of those dances, in front of him a little hole was hollowed out in the ground and those enjoying his music were expected to drop a coin in this hollow. One night an officer and a soldier from the local barracks appeared at one of those dances, they stood and observed the festivities. The officer had noticed a good looking girl, leaving the other soldier in charge of his horse, he asked her to dance. She danced with him for the rest of the night and he seemed to enjoy her company. As he was leaving he handed her a half sovereign for being so courteous, she thanked him but said it should go to the piper for providing the entertainment during the night. Her generosity to the piper impressed him, it was said that next day her family received a visit from the local landlord who told them that due to their daughter's good nature he would let them have the land free for half a year.

The Pattern in Dunmore is one of the best local heritage sites in Dunmore parish, in one small area there are seven items that form what is locally known as The Pattern

1. Tobar na Croise Naofa, Well of the Holy Cross, this is reputed to have cures and to have been blessed by St. Patrick.
2. A horseshoe shaped structure which is an outdoor altar where mass was celebrated or the rosary recited by the priest.
3. A small rectangular enclosure at the foot of the ash tree, believed to have been built much later than the altar, there is no trace of a roof but it could have been roofed in bygone days. Some believe it was a vestry for the priest but as it is built over water many locals believe it is where baptisms took place.
4. Directly across the path from the altar is a four foot high mound of stones, known as The Dean's Grave. Near the top on the back of this structure is a large flat stone with the imprint of three crosses. When each person completes a round they pick up a small stone from the top of the Dean's grave and retrace the markings on the stone.
5. Cnoic an Damhsa was a triangular clearing about thirty yards above the well where dances were held, it was a central point for people in the local villages, mountain paths led to it from the Gortnalea side and the Cloonkeen side, it is now very overgrown with furze, heather and hawthorn.
6. The Ash Tree, tales abound in the locality about this tree, the well is located near this tree.

7. The Pattern Road, which in reality is a country lane, leads from the village of Cappagh to Tobar na Croise Naofa and continues on past it.

One old local tale is about a man named Pettit, he tried to chop down the ash tree but a cross flew out of the trunk of the tree and according to local folklore, this cross hopped along the road until it came to rest in a monastery in Granlahan. Pettit was so terrified that he fled into town, just over two miles away, but his mind was deranged by the time he reached Dunmore.

Another more recent story concerned a local man who chopped a branch from the ash tree for firewood and one night as his wife sat beside the fire her leg was badly burned. Many people in Dunmore today remember that the burn on her leg never healed properly. Medicine today would no doubt have an explanation for the fact that her burn did not heal, but the story has gone into the legend of the Ash tree.

The Pattern Road was built in the 1930's as part of a work scheme. These work schemes were introduced during a time of high unemployment to provide work for men so they could earn "a few bob" to help them support their families. Pat Coleman from Cappagh was the "ganger" on the Pattern work scheme; his son Bertie, well known in GAA circles had the account books for this job. Sixty pounds was the amount of money allocated for constructing the road, drains and fences surrounding it. The men worked six days a week, eight hours a day and they received four shillings per day. Taking into account the conversion from the old pound to the punt and then onto the euro that would probably be in today's currency.. €1.50 per week. Pete Tierney who lived in Cappagh at the time told me about his time working on the road as a young man. Pete had a horse and cart, and wages were higher for the use of a horse and cart. He received nine shillings per day on the days he was allowed to bring his horse and cart to work. Carts were not needed every day, but when they were required there was great competition among those who owned them to see who would get to bring their horse and cart. Just reflect on the wages for a moment and you will notice that the horse's labour was worth a shilling more than a man.

Pete Tierney's nephew Johnny Mullarkey still lives in Cappagh and has many good stories about the village and the Pattern. St. Patrick is supposed to have visited Tobar na Croise Naofa in the Pattern on his journey from Mayo to the village of Shrule in Dunmore. John McLoughlin from Caramana told me the following story about St. Patrick's trip to Dunmore. While travelling through Mayo, St. Patrick was jeered by some young fellows and they also pelted clods of earth at him. He lost his temper and put a curse on them, now we must remember Patrick was not a saint at this time, he was a mere mortal like the rest of us, so we can understand why he might lose his temper when riled. By the time he reached Dunmore he was sorry he had cursed the Mayo boyos, so he decided to remove the curse. However, removing a curse was not a simple matter, he just couldn't just get rid of it, he had to transfer it to something else. He noticed that there were plenty of rushes growing around him so he put the curse on the rushes and that's why if you take the time to examine a rush, you will notice that the top of it is dead. St Patrick was standing in a village not far from Tobar na Croise Naofa when the idea struck him about how to remove the curse. The village of

Lisduff is unofficially known as Loorha and the word Loorha is an anglicised version of the Irish word for rushes… Luachra.

While a small number of people from the local villages of Cappagh, Gortnalea and Cloonkeen continued through the years to visit the Pattern, the practise in general began to die out in Dunmore. On 25th July, 1973, the Heritage committee with the help of Fr Williams revived the practise and mass was once again celebrated at the Pattern of Tobar na Croise Naofa. Mary Connolly sister of John McLoughlin wrote a poem about the Pattern after this event and it was published in the Tuam Herald.

Monsignor Michael Walsh carried on the tradition of Pattern Sunday and on the last Sunday in July he would recite the rosary while the gathering did the "rounds". This involves walking around the well, vestry and ash tree while the rosary is being recited. Everybody picks up a small rock which lays on top of the "Deans Grave" and retraces the markings on the flat stone on the back of this rectangular structure, this action is repeated each time a "round" is completed. The practise lapsed for a few years but Fr. John Cosgrove revived the tradition and had benediction and the rosary at the Pattern. One year a procession of people walked from the Abbey in Dunmore, down the Cloonfad Road turned left into Cappagh and up the Pattern road to Tobar na Croise Naofa. Local people including sisters Mary Teresa Reilly and Carmel Daniels (who grew up in the Bownes household in Cappagh and have now returned from London to live in Dunmore) decorate the area with pots of flowers for Pattern Sunday. In recent years it was also necessary for Fr Cosgrove to bring a container of holy water to place in the well. Due to an over enthusiastic cleanup of the area some years ago, a stream leading from the well was cleared out with a mechanical digger and the water hasn't appeared in the well since except in times of heavy rain.

Throughout the years people reminisced during the gathering about Pattern Sunday of their youth. Delia Flaherty from Drimbane told me that a large contingent from her village Cloonkeen used to make the pilgrimage to the Pattern, they had a pathway that they followed down Slieve Dart. She said seven "rounds" were made of the Deans Grave and seven "rounds" were made of the well and the altar, the Lords Prayer and the Hail Mary were recited seven times as the "rounds" were made. Many people finished the ceremony by standing in the well and reciting these prayers seven times. During the recent years the procession often became a little congested as everyone queued to mark the stone. In olden times three different groups would be walking simultaneously doing different "rounds" and movement was smoother.

Mick Costello remembered Joe Tracey telling him the story of his young brother, who had never walked. One Pattern Sunday his mother took this young lad along to the ceremony, she left him sitting on a smooth patch of ground below the well as she did the "rounds". When she was on the high spot near the Dean's Grave she glanced down to check if he was all right. She was amazed to see him making an attempt to walk; this was witnessed by all present. From that day onwards the boy walked, his gait wasn't perfect but he managed to get around.

With the shortage of clergy throughout Ireland, and our own parish now having only one priest and three churches, it is hard to continue on the tradition, but anybody can lead the rosary, so hopefully we will witness a few more Pattern Sundays.

FEMALE ENTREPRENEURS

Head scarfed women came on their bicycles-
at a time when there was no sell by dates or
preservatives, shopping bags brimming
with free range eggs and salty yellow butter
the eggs and butter a form of cash
bartered for bread, sugar, tea and groceries
to supplement the family income-
demand was great for their deliveries.

Hens and churning was seen as women's work-
at a time when food was as simple as life
but had almost disappeared by the middle of
the twentieth century when fork and knife
was relinquished to the finger and thumb
and a fast food nation we had become.

DUNMORE'S HERITAGE TREE

"I think that I shall never see
A poem as lovely as a tree"
So wrote Joyce Kilmer in days of yore
A sentiment not understood by some in Dunmore
When boughs were butchered from our Heritage Tree

"Poems are made by fools like me
But only God can make a tree"
This belief architect J.F. McCormack had as his core
When he designed the new vocational school in Dunmore
Slaughtered or salvaged by a committee, our Heritage Tree

In the early 1950's architect J.F. McCormack was appointed to draw up plans for the new vocational school to be built in Dunmore. This was the start of a new era for Dunmore, the construction of its first second level school. The site for the new school was on the outskirts of the town, on the Tuam road and located on the edge of Dunmore Demesne. The Demesne was a beautiful area that contained many mature and striking trees including chestnut and beech. Today environmental awareness is an issue usually taken into consideration during construction work but in those days it was not always an issue foremost in people's thoughts. J.F. McCormack was clearly a forward thinking individual, as there was an exceptionally beautiful beech tree that he wanted to preserve on the site donated by the Demesne committee for the vocational school "The tech was designed around that tree" is a phrase I have heard repeated over the years. Indeed the beech tree can be seen towering over the school in an article on Dunmore, that the GAA club placed in the front page of the Irish Independent in 1953.

Some years later the new Church was built in Dunmore across the road from the vocational school. As you exit the church the most prominent image in your sight is the towering beech tree. This icon of Dunmore has watched over the joy of weddings, confirmations and first communion ceremonies and it has watched over the heartache of funerals. Throughout the years of St. Patrick's Vocational School this tree has been an overhead shelter and undercover agent to the hopes and expectations of so many students. During his time as caretaker of the vocational school Paddy Glennon used to take great pride in keeping the area around the tree in immaculate condition, he often had fantastic borders of flowers surrounding this tree.

This was our Dunmore Heritage Tree, it was so much part of our community that we no longer saw it. It was there before we were born and would be there long after we all departed. It had many more years of life to observe in Dunmore. One Friday evening recently as I drove into Dunmore, in that time between twilight and night light, something was missing; I slowed down the car and reversed back. There was our Heritage Tree with its limbs hacked off and they lay scattered all round its trunk, strewn across the garden. The yellow metal ogre that executed the mutilation now lay in slumber in the darkness, and nobody around to question about this despoilment of this beautiful tree.

Next day I made enquiries for the reason this operation of mutilation took place. I didn't come up with any answers as I was referred from Billy to Jack to Jane and back to Billy. I know there is a committee who are trying to save the vocational school building and they deserve appreciation and help with this worthy task. I have also served on enough committees over the years to know how much unappreciated work committees carry out in communities. I heard a rumour that the tree was in bad condition and needed to be cut back to save it but the cutting back went nearer to cutting down and I am not the only person to believe it, there is no sign of decay visible on the tree. Another tree on the left hand side of the vocational school was completely chopped down and from the remains of its trunk this tree was also in perfect health. Communities are paying thousands of euros to plant large trees in their environs and in Dunmore we are paying wood butchers to chop down our mature trees. Its obvious that the vocational school is in a derelict condition but the splendour of the trees was concealing this, screening this dereliction from view. Now as you exit the church or enter Dunmore we have a clear unobstructed view of the dereliction. When the vocational school is renovated it will be an excellent addition to the community but the unique feature of this site has been destroyed. The tree now stands at about the same height as it did in 1953, it will hopefully recover but nobody living in Dunmore today will ever see the former magnificent lofty composition of our Heritage Tree, in their lifetime.

After Mass on that April Sunday 2011, following the destruction of the trees, the reaction was not good as people gazed with dismay on the scene before their eyes. I overheard part of a conversation between two men who I would imagine were past pupils of the school… "Who do you think did that, they destroyed the place, didn't they know the school was built around that tree?

HIGH HOPES

It was her old woman's legs that I first noticed about her as a child. Even today, her image comes easily to mind. Her thick black stockings covered layers of surplus flesh about her ankles. With her dyed black hair tied neatly in a bun, she continued to wear the traditional black clothing of a widow, even though her husband had died many years previously.

Mrs Nolan (called Bridget by her friends) always sat in the same place in her village country shop. Her chair was outside the counter, facing the entrance door. In Summer, the door was permanently open and Bridget saw most of what happened on the Main Street. When a customer entered to buy provisions, Bridget left her chair and waddled behind the counter. While she served some fresh sausages, half a pig's head, white loaves or loose tea and sugar, Bridget heard and reciprocated with the latest village news. This news was seldom of such high intrigue as to be considered scandal; it was simply gossip that fed the social appetites of the inhabitants. Mrs Nolan was friendly with many of the women in the village, who appreciated her ability to lend an ear to their problems and to give sound advice.

One early Summer evening, her neighbour and friend from across the street called over. Bridget saluted Kate warmly. They chatted about the recent spell of good weather that was sure to benefit the local farmers and ultimately the shopkeepers. As Bridget wrapped the bread, she said quietly.

"I had a visitor yesterday, Kate."
"Who was that, Bridget?" It was a routine response.
"Oh, it was a young woman. She asked about you and Michael. In fact, she asked about the two lads as well."
Bridget glanced down and pretended to busy herself with the twine. She tied more unnecessary knots around the brown paper parcel.

Kate's heart skipped a beat and sudden hope soared. Could it have been her daughter? The vivid, painful memories of her last night at home returned and she shivered as she recalled the episode. It was ten years ago, yet it seemed like yesterday. Alice, her eldest child had admitted one evening, after the family rosary, that she was pregnant. She was seventeen years old and had been seeing a local lad who was attending the technical school. Her husband Michael had flown into an unholy rage at the sudden shame that had descended upon his family. Kate had tried to restrain him, as he assaulted their daughter with his leather belt. He roared at her to leave his house and never to return.

Alice fled in fear and terror. At the front door she ran straight into the arms of Bridget who had heard the commotion and was on her way to investigate. Kate remembered the kindness of her neighbour who had given Alice shelter that night and money and provisions the following morning as she left on the bus for the ferry to England.

She had no communication with her daughter in the intervening years. Every night since, Kate had prayed for her return. Now perhaps she had come home. She could no longer restrain her high hopes.

"Bridget, was it Alice?" Kate asked her friend directly. Bridget raised her eyes and looked at Kate, shamefaced.

"She stood just inside the door. She called me by name, Kate and asked me if I remembered her. I couldn't admit that I didn't know her, so I pretended and said yes. I though her name would come before she left. We never finished her conversation, as Mrs O'Regan and her daughter came into the shop. The woman stood back while they came to the counter. When I turned around again, she had gone."

Bridget looked at her friend. Kate's disappointment was obvious as she sought to control her tears.

"I'm sorry Kate. I thought I should tell you. Maybe… she'll come back again?"

1979

Gloria was advising us "To Take One Day At A Time". Brendan Shine was asking "Do You Want Your Old Lobby Washed Down?" and The Village People were saying "It's Fun To Stay At the YMCA, Ami Stewart was singing "Knock on Wood" and Donna Summers, "Hot Stuff", thirty two years ago in 1979.

Gina Dale Haze and The Champions were Ireland's top pop group. Kramer V Kramer with Dustin Hoffman and Meryl Streep and The Deerhunter were two of the must see films while Sophie's Choice was "the" book.

The seventies generally was the disco craze decade. The ladies in particular dazzled and shimmered under the flashing lights with gold, silver and pink eye shadow while going bare faced (make-up free) during the day. Fashionable for boys were sports jackets and cost approximately £17.00. Often these were worn so frequently that wear and tear on the elbows necessitated the sewing on of leather patches.

In 1979 Sony introduced the Walkman to the market. This was a portable tape player and radio with ear phones and proved a popular Christmas gift that year. Black and Decker produced a cordless mini vacuum called the "Dust- Buster".

A new house in Galway city cost in the region of £18,000. A flashy wedding cost the equivalent of £4,000. Newly weds could buy 100% wool blankets for £11.99 and a set of towels for £1.99. A loaf of bread cost 59 pence, a pint cost 70 pence and a gallon of petrol was 79 pence, even though a crisis in the Middle East led to petrol shortages in May and long delays at garages across the country. A second oil crisis in 1979 plunged the western world into the worst recession since before World War II.

RTE 1 (Radio Telifis Eireann) opened at five in the evening, Monday to Friday and at eleven in the morning on Saturday and Sunday with Cartoon Time. RTE 2 opened at seven in the evening. Broadcasting ended just before or at midnight each night. Popular programmes at the time included, Man from Atlantis, Mork and Mindy, Hawaii Five O and Little House on the Prairie.

1979 was the year I did my Leaving Certificate in Scoil Chriost an Ri (Mercy Convent) Boyle. Thirty five thousand and five hundred and ten students sat the exam that year. This was two hundred and ninety four less than in 1978. However, the number of girls sitting the Leaving increased by three hundred and three while the number of boys decreased by five hundred and ninety seven on the previous year.

Even though a large number of students obtained the quota of four honours for University the majority opted for technical colleges and other higher education institutes. It was felt job opportunities were more likely with a qualification from these institutions than with an Arts degree. There was a limited number of teaching job vacancies in Ireland at this time.

The Banks and Civil Service claimed a large percentage of the school leavers. Many started nurse training and the army and navy were expanding their cadetships. However the people who left school in 1979 (myself included) were in competition with a backlog of students from 1978 who were on waiting lists for nurse training and cadetships. Some of us "took the boat" to Britain to further our education and find work.

Between January and March of 1979, PAYE workers in Ireland took to the streets protesting against the tax system. Dublin saw one of the largest anti PAYE demonstrations. 1979 was the worst year ever in Ireland for industrial disputes.

Jack Lynch, leader of Fianna Fail retired from politics and was replaced by Charles Haughey. In Britain, Margaret Thatcher made history when she became the first female prime minister in the United Kingdom.

The McCarthy cup went to Kilkenny that year when they defeated Galway. Sam went back to Kerry who defeated Dublin. Roscommon were the National League champions for the first time having beaten Cork in the final. They were in the top three football teams in the country, were under 21 champions and had three Connacht titles in a row.

In 1979 hurling lost the great Christy Ring, R.I.P., of Cork aged 58 years.

Mother Teresa of Calcutta received the Peace Prize. In August the first group of Vietnamese refugees arrived in Ireland and in September Pope John Paul II visited these shores. Two hundred and eighty five thousand attended the youth rally in Galway and three hundred thousand more flocked to Knock. Similar crowds saw him in the Phoenix park, Clonmacnoise, Maynooth, Drogheda and Limerick.

1979 saw the lowest temperatures of the twentieth century in Ireland. Recorded on January 2nd in Kildare, -18.8 degrees celsius.

TELEPHONES

I remember the day my best friend Ann got the telephone into their home. It got pride of place in the parlour. It was about 1970 and a most exciting time. Having a home telephone in the 1970's was a rarity in the West of Ireland. There was one public kiosk in the village and this served the limited needs of the local population. Since very few people had a telephone, having to use the public phone usually indicated some sort of emergency, calling the Doctor, the Vet or relatives in England to inform them of some catastrophe that could not await the usual method of communication, a letter.

The telephone kiosk was a yellow tall narrow structure with three walls of Georgian glass and one solid wall where the telephone hung. It was situated conspicuously on the outside of the footpath. To make a call you had to lift the big black hand piece, wind a leaver and wait to communicate with the local exchange. Then you had to say what number you wanted. The telephonist would tell you to hang up and she would ring you back with the number. While awaiting the call to come through it was advisable to have coins at the ready to put into the slots before you could talk to the person on the other end. When, eventually, the phone would ring the telephonist would tell you she had your number on the line and to insert the required amount of money and press button A. Button A accepted the coins while button B returned any unused coins. When you got through to the person on the other end of the line a chat would ensue. Sometimes you would get great value out of the coins inserted and other times the telephonist would interrupt the conversation telling both parties to get off the line or pay extra money. I remember one time when a particularly juicy piece of gossip was being discussed, the telephone crackled with a big intake of breath and an "O MY God" from a third party on the line. I'm not at all sure who the third party was but it always seemed that the local postmistress knew every titbit of news from both home and away.

My friend Avril had a telephone in her home. It was installed in the sitting room. It was the same as the phone in the kiosk and you had to insert the required amount of coins to make any call. Her much older brother was in America and doing very well we were informed, so they needed a telephone to keep in contact with him. I still remember their number, this number had a mere three digits, 128. I could not wait to get to the kiosk, about fifty yards away form Avril's house, to use the phone to ring her. It was such a thrill.

When I entered senior cycle in secondary school it was expected that each pupil would have some idea of what kind of work they would like to do after finishing school. Many of the girls in the class wanted to be nurses, others wanted to work in an office, and some aspired to be a telephonist. A telephonist at that time was a good permanent job. It was a prestigious job and many school girls dream career after completing the leaving cert.

Acquiring the telephone was a very onerous task. You applied for the phone, paid for the connection and then waited and waited. It usually took a good local TD to get it connected after years of waiting.

Years later – I would say around 1990 I got a telephone into my own house. Even at that time it was regarded as a bit of an extravagance but since other members of the family had installed their own it was very useful. By then you could dial the number required as the system had become automated.

As I recall, it was the mid 1990's by the time mobile phones became popular in Ireland. In 2000 the first mobile phone came into our house for my eldest son's sixteenth birthday. It was a big deal and he promised he would never ask for anything again. If only... The second mobile phone to enter our house was about one year later... for my daughter's birthday. Then my husband and I decided we would acquire one each, it would be handy for keeping in touch with the children. I can say that since the day I got my mobile phone I have become terribly attached to it. So much so that I cannot go anywhere without it by my side. If, by some terrible twist of fate, I end up phoneless for a day, I feel lost, that something is missing and I keep reaching for it without thinking. That's an addiction I've just described. It's not that I use it all that much, there are days that I don't use it at all! But I must have it with me to feel secure.

Surely the telephone has been one of the greatest inventions of all time. Today's phones are more gadget than phone and I would not change that. It beats standing in the kiosk.

AGGIE

The woman closed her eyes and exhaled a long breath. It was a two hour journey by train to Castlebridge. Last minute passengers crowded the aisles of the carriages and eventually found seats as the train pulled slowly out of Connolly station. Roberta settled into her seat, relieved that the long hours she had worked to complete the business project had finally come to an end. She smiled to herself as she thought of the incredulous looks she received from her colleagues earlier, when she excused herself from the celebration dinner and told them of her plans to spend the weekend in a little seaside village.

The train passes through small commuter towns before travelling through the rich farmlands of the midlands. It was late Autumn, but signs of Summer still lingered in neat fields and orchards. Hedgerows bounded the railway tracks where over-ripe fruit swung from desiccated stalks and trees clung stubbornly to their dried, withered leaves.

Roberta's thoughts wandered, as she mused about her relationship with Paul over the past two years. Paul had protested when she told him that she was spending the coming weekend alone, but Roberta ignored his muttering and grumbling until he eventually agreed.

There were times when she wished secretly that she had the courage to end their relationship. Paul had proposed marriage on more than one occasion, but still she hesitated without really analysing the reason for her refusals.

And now, she had another reason to seriously consider her future. Roberta was two months pregnant, but she had not yet told Paul. The question was, did she really want to continue with this pregnancy, which was totally unplanned? Roberta pushed these thoughts firmly aside, when finally the train stopped in Castlebridge. There was plenty of time to consider her options over the coming weekend.

She stepped down lightly from the train and sought directions to her accommodation from another traveller. It was a short walk to her destination and within ten minutes she was knocking on the door of Aisling House. The owner welcomed Roberta, and showed her to a room overlooking a beautiful manicured garden to the rear of the house. Her host introduced herself as Angela Donagehy and offered her visitor a cup of coffee, which Roberta gratefully accepted. After she thanked Angela, Roberta enquired about local walks around the area. "If you want to walk this evening, it would be best if you took the left path at the end of Church Street," she said, then added. "The County Council are undertaking some repair work near the shore, but there are plenty of nice walks behind the village towards the town, I suggest you go in that direction."

Roberta set out determined to have a brisk walk before dinner. At the Church Street junction, she hesitated and looked at the sky; it was clear with no signs of rain. She reckoned that she would have at least one hour walking before dusk. Ignoring Angela's advice, Roberta turned right in the direction of the beach.

The tide had receded, leaving unblemished white sand that enveloped her shoes with a soft welcome. Roberta walked on enjoying the smell and sound of the sea and soon passed the boulders where workers had erected warning signs of work in progress. She paid little attention to the wind, which was now gaining strength and bent her head against the force. Lost in thought, Roberta suddenly realised that someone was walking close beside her. She glanced quickly at her companion. It was an elderly woman, dressed in an old fashioned cross over apron over a black serge dress. She wore a headscarf tied in the traditional manner and her thick brown stockings were crumpled above her sensible laced shoes.

"Good evening Miss," Roberta said, but the woman made no reply. Oh well, Roberta shrugged mentally, perhaps she's deaf. Or maybe she's just a little odd. For whatever reason, the woman seemed happy to continue in silence. And so, for a short period of time, both walked together. Roberta, her head still bent against the wind, resumed her reverie, but a sudden splatter of cold rain quickly roused her from her daydream. She looked to the suddenly dark and menacing clouds, then towards her companion, but the woman had departed as silently as she had appeared. Roberta quickly turned in the direction of the Guest House. Angela opened the door at her arrival and looked at her bedraggled guest.

"You got caught in that shower," she said, stating the obvious. Roberta smiled. "It's nothing that a hot shower won't fix she replied. Angela nodded in agreement.

"What direction did you go?". Roberta told her and then as Angela turned to go, Roberta stopped her with a question.

"Do you know most people around the village, Angela?" she enquired. "Yes," she replied. I've lived here all my life. Why do you ask?"

Roberta described the woman who had joined her for part of the walk. As she spoke, Angela looked at her curiously. She was silent a moment and then said slowly. "That was old Mrs Griffin. I didn't know her personally, but my mother remembered her. She lived up the road; you passed her house on the way to the beach".

"Lived? Roberta interrupted her quickly." "Yes, she died in the fifties," Angela said quietly. I think you met a ghost, Roberta. Poor Aggie, she was a widow for many years. She never had children and died alone.

Roberta felt hairs stand erect on her neck and her knees suddenly seemed about to collapse. Angela looked at her white face and quickly helped her guest onto the nearest available chair. Angela took a couple of moments to recover and then looked over at her host.

"Tell me more, please" she requested, "about that poor woman."

Angela replied. "I really don't know a great deal about her, but rumour has it that Aggie once had a baby, who died shortly after birth. In those times, if a baby wasn't baptised, they were not buried in consecrated ground in the local graveyard. Babies lived in limbo and could never get to heaven. They were excluded in this life and in the next. The strange thing is, Angela continued "Aggie was never seen before last month, when the workmen began repairing the walkway that collapsed. The old people claim there is an unmarked graveyard near that spot for miscarried and unbaptised babies. My own belief is that Aggie has come back now to protect her baby's grave from the threat of danger."

Roberta thanked her host for the story. Long after she had retired for the night, her thoughts returned to the woman who had walked silently by her side. She had never believed in ghosts. But now... was there another message just for her? It was probably a fanciful idea from a pregnant woman, but she thought Aggie was making a silent plea for another unborn child. Before dawn came she had made up her mind to share her news with Paul. She hoped she would do as good a job as Aggie in protecting her future baby.

SEASONS IN THE BOG

Bog sleeps in waiting
Pale ghostly grass lying limp
Red moss mounds sodden

Brown and buff decaying stuff
Seek the vernal equinox

Spring sap is rising
Tadpoles dance in dark pools
Beside cotton clouds

Fresh heavy sods flung from slean
Firm up light in Summer air

Turf harvest moving
Curlews call and skylark sing
Tractors trundle home

Then autumn heath and heather
Silver birch and snipe abound

Winter sleep begins

BEEHIVES, BOUFFANTS AND BOWLCUTS

Jedward, our Eurovision representatives this year, are as famous for their huge hair, as for their singing. High hair in general previously popular in the 60's and 80's is making a comeback.

Since prehistoric times (from hair to eternity!) people have changed their hair (some overnight) by cutting it, dyeing it, adding curls and/or straightening it, among other things! When babies get their first haircut the mother (usually) saves a lock of the hair and holds on to it as a keepsake. A trip to the hairdressers is a treat for most people and regardless of economic downturn hairdressing remains big business. It would be fair to say that hair has a history.

Hairstyles change regularly with a lot of hairstyles that are "in" today originating in the 1900's. In Victorian times ladies didn't cut their hair and they tended to wash their hair once a month or less. The "Roaring 1920's" saw ladies abandon the constraints of Victorian life and follow trends set by their screen idols in cinema and theatre. Hair washing was done more frequently and by the 1950's people generally were washing their hair once a week. Today daily hair washing is quite common.

Short, bobbed and wavy hairstyles represented independence and freedom of spirit among women. They were kept neat through the wearing of hair-nets. At the same time as different hairstyles emerged so did the use of face powder, rouge and very red lips. Do you remember the page boy hairstyle for ladies? A style first worn by Gretta Garbo.

Men's hair in the 20's was short, with a centre parting and slicked back with Brilliantine and perfumed oils. The "short back and sides" military style haircut with a few variations has remained fairly constant throughout the years for men.

During World War 1 French women (trend-setters in fashion even then!) began working outside the home. They did jobs that were previously classed as men's work. The Bob hairstyle was practical for these women. There was the classic Bob and the Shingle Bob, the latter having a v shape cut at the back of the neck.

Various styles of the Bob remained popular in the 1930's and 1940's. Women continued to work during the Depression and World War II on farms and industry (munitions factories) and they needed short easy to care for styles. Wealthier women went for longer, soft curl styles.

The 1940's however saw a trend in more romantic styles. Soft curls to the shoulders or a long naturally wavy look. Sun tans became popular in the 1940's, again following their own screen idols.

During the war hairstyles were dictated by practicality. Shampoo was hard to come by, and because of the type of work women did short styles were popular, especially during the day. Some wore their hair in a neat roll, over their ears around the nape of their necks for practicality, and then let it hang down loose for night time. A popular trend was to cover hair with headscarves knotted at the front leaving only the fringe exposed.

Post war and in the 1950's women had more time to care for their hair so longer hair became the "in thing". Ladies at this time were craving glamour. It was in the 1950's that hair care products became available, and as a result more elaborate styles. Hair was abused, permanently waved and sprayed. The shampoo and set started.

The first hairdryer apparently was a vacuum cleaner adapted for drying hair. A man called Godfrey invented the first hairdryer in 1890. Hairspray in cans, shampoo, conditioner and rollers became big business that boomed in the 1960's. Young girls tied their hair up in a ponytail and more mature "girls" had a French pleat. The Pixie style, similar to how Audrey Hepburn wore hers, short with a short fringe was "in" then.

Before shampoo became widely available people boiled soap in water. Talc was often used to absorb excess oil in the hair. Carbolic soap with it's distinctive smell and Lifebuoy was used extensively in homes, hospitals, schools and farms on every type of surface including hair!

It was towards the end of the 50s and the early 1960's that the complex Beehive and Bouffant styles became popular. They were the start of "the big hair" days which is becoming popular once again. A variation on these was a half up half down style, that is favourable with girls at school graduations. The Beehive was hair which was backcombed and sprayed with hairspray into a big mound that resembled a beehive. Do you remember Dusty Springfield's beehive?

The men of the '50's slicked back their hair with the Brilliantine into a wavy quiff with big long sideburns. At the back the hair was combed back to meet in the middle and the comb was ran down the centre. It resembled a duck's tail or as some people called it a "Duck's Arse" haircut. Men copied James Dean and Elvis Presley. Tony Curtis was popular on screen at the time and this hair cut was often called a Tony Curtis cut. The Pompadour cut like what Johnnie Cash had, was another popular style.

Blonde was the colour in the sixties. A lot of women worked outside of the home in this decade and short back combed hair with a fringe was popular, sprayed with the inevitable hairspray to stay in place. Pony tails with a ribbon was favoured by those who liked long hair and when going out a night they left the hair loose. Highlights grew in popularity around then and gave that sun-kissed look. Many girls soaked strands of hair in lemon juice and sat in the sun.

Long hair for men in the '60's and 70's was a symbol of rebellion against the cultural norm. The opposite was true for the girls, who cut their hair very short and/or spiky. The Shag hairstyle was what the Beatles had and again as their popularity grew so did this style of haircut.

The 70's was the era for long, free and natural styles. "Manes" of free falling curls with a soft fringe or a parting was the way to go! Charlie's Angels were the trend setters in this era. Soft, flowing, parted in the centre or just off centre and teased back from the face with dryer and brush or curling tongs.

Some men went for layers and feather like cuts. Others rebelled during the punk years where spiked, dyed fluorescent colours were all the rage.

The Perm took off in the early '80's in both women and men. A pressing and curling iron was invented by Stephens in the late eighties. I remember getting my hair "crimped" with a crimping machine in 1983. I had naturally curly hair so as you can imagine when it was "crimped" and straightened in the space of an hour I had gained inches of extra hair. It was acceptable though because the '80's was the era of "big hair"!

It was in the '80's that hair products specifically for men flooded the market. Up until then they had to do with a very limited choice unless they "borrowed" from their sister, girlfriend or in some instances their mother.

Keeping with the "big hair" trend the '80's saw the arrival of the Afro hairstyle regardless of ethnicity or sex. Men and women went into the hairdressers with an average six inches of hair and emerged two hours later with a halo of curly hair.

A choppy, highlighted cut resembling Madonna followed for "the girls" and a style called the Bowl cut for "the boys". This was exactly what it said and resembled as if someone had put a bowl on your head and cut around it. Needless to say this style didn't last.

From the 1990's up until the present time has been the era of "the anything goes trend" in hair styling. Long and sleek with long layers, blonde, highlighted, worn long or short. Extensions, mousse, anti frizz agents and of course the hair "straightener" have become some of the current must haves.

For men shaved heads where anything over an inch was considered long remains popular. The close shave at the sides and a scissor cut on top is now "in" but if the history of hairstyles is anything to go by a new trend will emerge. Perhaps in the guise of the Mullet. This style is short in front and long at the back and sometimes a long strand is left at the back aptly named "a tail". This style has reared it's "head" every now and then over the last thirty years.

SCHOOL DAYS

Yesterday my friend produced out of her handbag a packet of sweets. These sweets were no ordinary sweets, they were hard juicy and eye rollingly delicious sweets, just like the sweets of my childhood. In fact it brought me right back to being in Infants class, to a day I was feeling ill and the teacher told me to come and sit on the sweet can by the fire.

Before I sat on the can she opened it and told me to have a magic sweet which would make me better. I looked into the sweet can and my mouth watered with the array of beautifully presented sticky hard sweets, some were yellow some black and more were red with white stripes. I took one and savoured its delicious flavour while sitting by the open turf fire on the sweet can. This delicious delicacy certainly did have healing properties as I was feeling better in no time.

Before going to school my mother would have porridge ready for breakfast.
I consumed this with very little relish and tried to make it more palatable by adding sugar, lots of it, and milk. In order to arrive at school on time mother insisted that we leave the house each morning when the Lyons Tea advertisement came on the radio. It was always broadcast at 8.40am. So out the back door I skipped to the refrain, "Buy Lyons Tea, The Quality Tea, The Quality Tea, Buy Lyons Tea, The Quality Tea, The Quality Tea. My school was two miles away from my home.

In order to reach the school it was necessary to walk the distance as there was no school transport in 1965. By road, the distance was two miles but we had a short cut across the fields, which reduced the distance to about one mile. Some mornings, in those early days, I being a little one would get a piggy back from the older children as I was halting their progress with little steps.

The shortened journey required that my brother and I walk through the fields of a neighbour. The big paddock was the first field, then into the well field and onto the neighbouring house where we joined three more children ready for school. From there we went on through the little paddock, onto the style field and into Griffin's field where we climbed over the ditch and joined the road before the wooden bridge.

There was a monster lurking underneath this bridge ready to devour everyone who lingered long enough to gaze into the deep choppy waters below. We hardly dared breathe as we raced across this bridge. I can still remember my heart pounding in terror in case that monster would come from the depths to devour us. I have a vivid image of what that monster looked like. He had long black hair sleeked onto his skull with big sunken eyes, hungry jaws and teeth ready to devour. He had very broad shoulders and was dressed in a black cape.

Once we got across the bridge we could breathe a sigh of relief. On we went to the main road. This was called the dark road as it was newly tarred and had a hard shoulder with three rows of cat's eyes. On this road we would invariably meet up with other pupils making their way to school. There were few enough cars going the way, and we always knew how early or late we were by where we were when the teacher's car passed us.

On that road it was usual to meet army lorries coming from Athlone. These lorries had canvas covering the back and the rear was open. I could see the soldiers sitting inside with guns by their sides. I waved and so did they. This was a game we played when we met the army lorries. We tried to get as many soldiers as we could to wave back to us. Eventually we arrived at school and commenced another day of learning and play.

For pupils in junior and senior infants school finished at 2pm and continued until 3pm for everyone else. This meant that the return journey home was undertaken by me and my neighbour Adam. We were both five years old and enjoyed each other's company no end.

We strolled along heedless of time as we chatted about my cat and his farm. During the hot weather I remember taking off my blue plastic sandals and my toes sticking into the bubbling tar. I also took great delight in walking through the fields in my bare feet as the grass had a lovely cooling effect.

When it rained I had my own black Dunlop Wellingtons. I wore these with great pride as they were one of the few possessions I had that had not belonged to someone else before me. We made the perilous return journey across the wooden bridge racing hand in hand to get to the other side. Once we had surmounted that obstacle we would slow to a stroll or even sit down for a rest.

As we travelled along the road we met neighbouring farmers. Each one would have the same questions to ask. "Did you learn much today?" and how many slaps did you get?". I being quiet shy would whisper "yes sir" and "no sir". Sometimes the older children would catch up with us on their way home and could not understand how we had not reached home yet. I remember Adam's mother told us that we had to be home before the older children or we would be in trouble. That improved our progress – a bit.

When we reached Adam's house I always went inside. His mother being a very kind lady, always gave me a cup of milk. This milk was produced on their own farm from their own cows. It was lovely. Sometimes she would give me a cut of homemade bread laced with thick creamy butter. This bread had a flavour all of its own and my mouth waters even now when I think of it.

In her kitchen she had a very large wooden box with a sloped lid on the top. I never got to look into this box and still wonder what it looked like inside. From this box she produced things like bread, butter, jam and flour.

I waited there until my brother Pat, who would have been in sixth class, got to their house and we resumed our journey across the last few fields and home. During the months of March, April and May my progress home was slowed down by the compulsion I had to pick flowers. Daffodils appeared during the month of March. I would pick a few and bring them home to my mother. She would have a jam jar ready to use as a vase and they would be displayed on the kitchen table.

On the first day of May we would erect a May altar. This was a special altar in honour of Our Lady. Her statue was the centre piece and jam jars of various sizes were filled with whatever flowers were available. Mary was circled with a garden of flowers for the full month of May and I was on flower picking duty.

I remember having a plentiful supply of primroses, daffodils, daisies, apple blossom, lilac, cherry blossom and blue bells. I remember the scent of each one, and still, love the sight of those coloured heads as they open to the sunshine.

This pattern continued until free school transport was introduced a few years later. I no longer crossed the fields and the freedom to stroll along and chat forever was gone, but I became familiar with a whole new bigger world.

THE ROAD THROUGH MUINÉEN RUA

By Michael Hannon

It was the road to nowhere.
The bog road through Muinéen Rua.
Constructed sometime around 1943
Or was it forty two?
We knelt on straw sheaves .
With hand held lump hammers.
Breaking stones –
Tick-tacking away like a fairy
shoemaker.
On a moonlight night.

We wore scratched goggles.
To shield our eyes from the splinters.
That now and then
Clipped us on the side of the ear.
Causing us to utter profanity
Under our breath.

Joe White and Mick Burke ,
Told tales of their time in England.
And the money they made.
Why did they not stay there, I asked myself?
For here in Muinéen Rua we toiled for a pittance.
A handout, on a road to nowhere,
... When the money ran out

Across the water in England
People were dying daily in air raids
Here in Muinéen Rua,
We were dying gradually from
the biting wind.
That swept across the bog from
Gurteen

We ate our dinner,
In a canteen built of bog scraws.
Glad of brief respite,
From the biting wid..
Tom Donnellon lit his pipe after
dinner.
And smoked in silence.
I pulled on a Woodbine butt.
That I had stacked away in the corner
Of an old Oxo tin .

We stopped work when the
Angelus bell ran.
Making the most of it.
Heads dropped like roses on wet day.
"God knows, ye must all be saints"
Said Pat Coleman, the ganger.
Wondering if we were ever
going to resume work.
Jim Fallon filled us in on life in America.

It wasn't Utopia for everyone he said,
And we believed him.
It wasn't Utopia here either.
For one pound sixteen and
four pence a week
Under our breath.

Kids today get more in pocket money
Than we did in wages.
Yet we survived the wind and weather
And all that life dished out.
Maybe Muinéen Rua had something
to do with it
After all.

I wanted to include this poem by my
Uncle Michael Hannon whose poetry
has been published in various
publications in Ireland, Britain and the
USA. He also had a poetry slot on the
Celtic Fringe programme on Radio
Leicester. I think this is one of his most
powerful poems, it tells of his time as a
young man working on one of the
work schemes in early 1940's.
You can feel the despondency of the men.

This road was in Muinéen Rua
(The Red Bog), which is located across the
bridge in front of John Fallon's house
on the Killooney/Ballinlass border
When the money ran out all work
would stop and the road would lead to
nowhere, similar to what happened on
The Pattern road some years earlier
the ganger on this job was also Pat Coleman.

FLYING HIGH

It was a damp, cold All Souls Eve when Maura Daly found herself on the N63 Roscommon to Galway road. The forecasted rain from the Atlantic was now crossing the country and the darkness that had been descending since early afternoon enfolded everywhere.

Maura was going to visit her Auntie Mai in the hospital and could just make out the distant lights of the city. Visibility generally was fairly poor. She did think of turning back but knowing Mai would be disappointed she struggled on. Her Auntie Mai was ninety three years old and still lived alone in a picturesque bungalow outside Ballygar. Maura was very fond of her Aunt and admired her. She had been admitted with a fractured wrist five days earlier. She had sustained the injury following her ninety third birthday celebrations. Auntie Mai insisted on having a birthday party every year. Maura had been "put in charge" of her five "babies" while she was in the hospital. The "babies" were a group of overfed and pampered cats, all of whom Mai had rescued at varying times over the years.

Thoughts of Mai and her cats forced her to smile. She turned on the radio in an attempt to drown out the constant sweep and swish of the windscreen wipers which had started to irritate her.

"What was that?" Maura let out a muted cry as something big and white flew across her windscreen at speed. By now she was approaching a small narrow bridge spanning the Clare river, somewhere between Abbeyknockmoy and Turloughmore. She braked sharply. Fortunately there was no one tailgating her.

"Please don't let me have hit anyone or anything". Maura implored as she indicated and pulled in on the hard shoulder. "Surely I'd have heard a noise or felt a bump if I had hit something" she attempted to reassure herself. "Probably just a plastic bag, one of those that farm supplies come in and that some people use for turf", she reassured herself. But no matter how much Maura tried to reason there was still a niggling voice in her head telling her different. It was just that it all happened so fast.

Did it have a face? She asked no-one in particular. She didn't think so but she couldn't be sure. She decided to take a look. Maura switched on the hazard lights on the car, grabbed the torch she kept under the passenger seat and swung herself reluctantly out into the damp air. Cars coming from Galway whizzed past. Outbound traffic was heavier than inbound at this time of the evening. Holding the lapels of her coat in an attempt to block out the bitter chill with one hand and holding the torch with the other hand she retreated to the spot where she believed she had seen it. In her three inch heels she had to zig zag through mud and slush to avoid the bigger pools of water on the road.

Surveying her surroundings the damp smell of the ditches wafted up her nostrils making her feel sick. She had a tight feeling in her head. She couldn't see a thing. Eyes darting she moved the beam of the torch to the left, nothing, back to the right, nothing. Then across the shadowy grass verge letting it rest on the stream, still nothing. She shivered as the cold wind drove the rain into her.

The gushing, murky water seemed to chuckle as it flowed. Was it gloating at her, Maura wondered as if at some secret joke. It was all very creepy and Maura didn't like it.

"Get a grip", she told herself. There's nothing here. A car slowed and its occupants stared out at her curiously. Another pulled up and enquired if she was all right. She hurriedly told them in a strange sounding voice that she was, well what else could she say?

"I think I saw something white fly across my windscreen but I don't know if I did, and I'm standing here in the driving rain looking for it. The next thing in white she'd see would be "the men in white coats" carting her away to the psychiatric ward. She hurried back to the car, hugging her shivering body with both hands as if to hold herself together.

Back in the warm cocoon of her car Maura grabbed the emergency pack of cigarettes from the glove box and lit up. She was in the early stages of giving up but had kept an emergency box "just in case". Well, this was an emergency and leaning back in her car seat she smoked two in quick succession lighting one from the other and gasping as the smoke hit the back of her throat and blazed a fiery trail down to her lungs.

No matter how she examined the events she couldn't seem to make sense of them. She was a secondary school teacher for God's sake. Her no nonsense attitude she always believed, was her key characteristic. She was capable of exerting control over a classroom of thirty odd teenage boys and girls and yet here she was quaking in her boots over a "white plastic bag". Funny, Maura thought how the smallest unforeseen event can bring about chaos and reduce a thirty something sensible human being into a scared, vulnerable one afraid of her own shadow in a matter of minutes.

She put the car into gear and drove off slowly, glancing furtively in the mirror several times. "Was it a sign, an omen? She wondered. "Was something wrong with Auntie Mai? She checked her mobile to see if the hospital had tried to get in contact with her. No message, no missed call. Concentrating hard on the road ahead and gripping the steering wheel as if her life depended on it she completed the rest of the journey sighing with relief as she saw the familiar grey of the cathedral in front of her.

As usual she had to circle the car park three times before she found a parking space and then it was a good distance from the main door. She grabbed the silver mints and mint aero chocolate bars (Mai's favourite things) off the back seat and hurried into the hospital. Wet and bedraggled she almost ran into the ward, glad for once of the extreme heat that met her. Usually she found it unbearable.

"Aunti Mai, sorry I'm late", she greeted the older woman.
"Maura alanna, are you alright? "You're very pale", Mai replied with her sharp all seeing eyes taking in every detail of the younger woman. "You look like you've seen a ghost".

At Mai's words Maura burst out laughing. She couldn't stop. All her earlier tension evaporated as the tears of laughter rolled down her cheeks. When she eventually stopped and gathered enough breath to reply she said "Maybe I have Mai, and in a voice thin with nerves she related the events of her evening.

"Now Maura alanna, you know there's no such thing as ghosts", Mai told her.

"Well that's what I used to think Auntie Mai, but now I'm not so sure".

VESSELS

The word vessel brings to mind
Memories from a distant time
When mother would say all in a flurry
Wash these vessels but do hurry

These things called vessels would include
The pots the pans the crock and can
Even the tin bath got a good rub
As we hustled and bustled
And everything in our midst got a scrub
As we finished the task
That always came in the way
Of more exciting outdoor play

Now I reflect and think it better
To encourage my own crew to declutter
The modern vessels of Xbox and Router
To regain more time to be with mother

Vessels awakens old memories
Of a time free from worries
When life was simple and times were good
And when water cleansed as it should
In vessels full to the brim with suds

Don't close the cover just yet!

The following three pages have entries from three guest poets;

My Bird by Maura Burke

Weight of the World by Brendan Finnegan

Haiku by Donal Finnegan

MY BIRD

He swoops down on the window sill as cocky as a prince

A little Willie Wag Tail, bold in self defence,

No other bird is welcome to invade his precious space,

His eyes are darting everywhere as he gulps his crumbs in haste,

His forked tail is wagging as he fills his little tum,

then he flies off to the nearest tree, his own sweet tune to hum.

When I look out in the morning, he is waiting on the wire,

I put out a fistful of breadcrumbs, before I light the fire.

WEIGHT OF THE WORLD

The weight of the world is on all our young

So much to plan for and so much to come

Try to plan for the future but you're in the past

Trying best to make the good times last

Well you've been to school and you know it all

Nothing to learn but how far we will fall

The Banks have the money and they're home and dry

The Tiger is dead and so is the high

We owe billions but we'll borrow some more

Make the children pay it off or show them the door

We're in this together and we can't get out

Just leave it to the rest to figure it out

They tax the poor to save the rich

Cut social pay ain't that a bitch

Enforce student fees and cut employees

But save themselves and their fancy cars

We've got no jobs or money

People on the streets can't even eat

It mightn't worry you but it gets to me

A safe future is only a dream.

HAIKU

White Suds on Water
Soap Messiah of hygiene
Rinse, Lather, Repeat

Haiku is a Japanese form of poetry consisting of three lines, unrhymed, of five, seven and five syllables. Haiku do not have a title and in their "pure" form reflect a moment of communion with nature.